Exploring
THE BIBLE

Ecclesiastes:
Joy that perseveres

A devotional commentary

Michael LeFebvre

DayOne

Endorsements

The one book of the Bible given to help us figure out life's painful riddles can itself be puzzling to those who study it. Yet with his customary clarity and exacting exegesis, Michael LeFebvre helps you see the big picture of Ecclesiastes in this devotional commentary. Through his doing so in a warm and winsome way, Ecclesiastes' message of enjoying God above everything else 'under the sun' is brought into sharp focus and ready applications.

Barry York, Professor of Pastoral Theology, Reformed Presbyterian Theological Seminary, Pittsburgh, Pennsylvania

A harbour of joy, a curriculum on delight, a melody of joy—not the kinds of phrases that usually come to mind when we think of Ecclesiastes. Which is why I'm delighted to see this important study by Dr Michael LeFebvre. As a first-rate pastor-theologian, Michael leads us through this hard-to-understand book with both scholarly heft and pastoral verve. This is devotional commentary writing at its best! I highly recommend it to pastors and preachers, students and scholars alike!

Dr Todd Wilson, Senior Pastor of Calvary Memorial Church, Oak Park, Illinois, Chairman of the Board for the Center for Pastor Theologians, and author

Ecclesiastes can be confusing. On the other hand, it is also piercingly honest. Dr LeFebvre helps us to see that while Ecclesiastes accurately records the contradictions and tensions we experience in life, the book itself does not contradict the overall message of the Scriptures. Instead, it leads us into wisdom and joy, in and through Jesus Christ. Highly recommended!

Dr Joel R. Beeke, President, Puritan Reformed Theological Seminary, Grand Rapids, Michigan

© Day One Publications 2015

ISBN 978-1-84625-463-5
All Scripture quotations, unless stated otherwise, are from the anglicized edition of
the ESV Bible copyright © 2002 Collins, part of HarperCollins Publishers.

British Library Cataloguing in Publication Data available

Published by Day One Publications
Ryelands Road, Leominster, HR6 8NZ
Telephone 01568 613 740 FAX 01568 611 473
email—sales@dayone.co.uk
web site—www.dayone.co.uk

North America—email—usasales@dayone.co.uk

Cover design by Rob Jones, Elk Design
Printed by TJ International

Dedication
For my children
and the youth of my congregation

Contents

Preface

Writing a commentary on Ecclesiastes is a risky undertaking. Few books of the Bible are as challenging and as open to different interpretations. Ecclesiastes is full of obscure Hebrew words, unusual turns of phrase, statements that seem to contradict one another, sudden leaps in thought from one subject to another, and numerous other features that make its study difficult.

Occasionally, one encounters high praise of the book, as that of the novelist Thomas Wolf: 'That book seems to me the noblest, the wisest, and the most powerful expression of man's life upon this earth ... Ecclesiastes is the greatest single piece of writing I have ever known.'[1] However, most people just find the book confusing.

Because Ecclesiastes is such a difficult book to study, perhaps it is best approached after the manner of a jigsaw puzzle. When solving a complicated jigsaw puzzle, one generally begins by finding the pieces with straight edges and assembling them into the frame. Once the borders are defined, figuring out how each piece fits becomes easier. Solving a jigsaw puzzle (or interpreting Ecclesiastes in this manner) can still be frustrating, but the task is aided by having a sense of the coherent structure into which the many oddly shaped pieces fit.

The present study of Ecclesiastes begins (in the Introduction) with attention to the 'big picture' structure of the book, and (in Chapter 1) with clues to the goals of the book in the way Ecclesiastes introduces itself. Orienting ourselves to the parameters and purposes of the book will aid in the task of assessing how each piece fits. That is the approach I have attempted in this study. But such an approach, while helpful, also has its dangers.

Beginning with the 'big picture' like this must be done carefully, in order not to ignore or to smooth out difficulties artificially. Most commentators agree that Ecclesiastes is by design full of contradictions and difficult sayings. Ecclesiastes is a study of life, and life is full of contradictions and confusion. Ecclesiastes honestly portrays the intransigent contradictions of life, not only in what it says but also in how it says it. When studying Ecclesiastes, a reader must hold in balance the conviction, on the one hand, that the book does have a coherent message; and the awareness, on the other hand, that the tensions within the book are part of the reading experience and must not be smoothed away.

I have endeavoured to maintain that balance in this study, but I will leave it to my readers to render their judgement of how well I have succeeded. The interpretation of Ecclesiastes is a difficult project; but the rewards of wrestling with this text far outweigh its challenges!

The studies contained in these pages took shape through a summer Bible study in my home and a later series of Sabbath School classes with my congregation. I want to thank the participants in that home Bible study for their contributions: Heather, Jacob, Debby, Christina, Rodrigo, Kevin, Amy, Esmiralda, Duane, Anne and Rutledge. I am also grateful for the thoughtful interaction of members of my congregation (Christ Church Reformed Presbyterian) in Sabbath School classes working through this material. Furthermore, I am thankful for the many commentators who have written on Ecclesiastes, from whose works I have drawn much assistance.[2]

None of these individuals should be blamed for errors I may have made, nor should any of them be presumed to agree with my conclusions. Nevertheless, all study of Scripture requires collaboration with others—especially study of a book as rich and complex as Ecclesiastes. I want to express my appreciation for the sharpening interaction of these fellow students of Ecclesiastes.

Michael LeFebvre

Brownsburg, Indiana, USA

Notes

1 Thomas Wolf, cited in Eric S. Christianson, *Ecclesiastes Through the Centuries* (Malden, MA: Blackwell, 2007), p. 70.

2 In particular, I have benefited from the following commentaries: Roland E. Murphy, *Ecclesiastes* (WBC 23A; Nashville: Thomas Nelson, 1992); Michael V. Fox, *A Time to Tear Down and a Time to Build Up: A Re-reading of Ecclesiastes* (Grand Rapids: Eerdmans, 1999); Robert Gordis, *Koheleth: The Man and His World* (Texts and Studies of JTSA, 19; New York: The Jewish Theological Seminary of America, am 5711/1951); Graham Ogden, *Qoheleth* (Sheffield: Sheffield Academic Press, 1987); James L. Crenshaw, *Ecclesiastes: A Commentary* (OTL; Philadelphia: Westminster Press, 1987); Doug Ingram, *Ambiguity in Ecclesiastes* (LHBOTS 431, New York: T&T Clark, 2006); Daniel C. Fredericks, 'Ecclesiastes', pp. 15–263 in Daniel C. Fredericks and Daniel J. Estes, *Ecclesiastes and the Son of Songs* (AOTC 16; Downers Grove, IL: InterVarsity Press, 2010).

Why study Ecclesiastes?

A ccording to an old Jewish tradition, Solomon wrote about romance in his youth (Song of Songs), and he wrote about parenting and business in his prime (Proverbs). Then, losing the optimism of his younger years, he wrote Ecclesiastes in the disillusionment of his old age.[1] This ancient tradition captures a sentiment still common today. Many think that Ecclesiastes is a book of despair, contradicting the hopeful tone of the other Solomonic wisdom books.

Ecclesiastes does admit that life is full of vanities. But that does not mean it is a book of despair. I believe it is a book of great hope. Ecclesiastes guides us through the vanities of life in order to teach us true joy in spite of them. Ecclesiastes is not a book of despair, but a book of realistic hope: realistic enough to face the worst of life's vanities and emerge rejoicing.

The book of Ecclesiastes is divided into six major sections.[2] In each of these six segments, the doubts and sorrows of life are rehearsed. But each of these excursions through murky waters ends at a harbour of joy. The close of each section is punctuated by the repeated chorus 'There is nothing better for a person than that he should eat and drink and find enjoyment in his toil. This also, I saw, is from the hand of God ...' (2:24–26; cf. 3:12–15; 5:18–20; 8:15; 9:7–10; 11:8). The wording varies slightly in each instance, but the repeated call to 'eat and drink *with joy*' emerges as Ecclesiastes' triumphant chorus.[3]

The importance of this theme is confirmed in the final chapter of the book. In its epilogue, Ecclesiastes describes itself as a book providing 'words of *delight,* and ... words of truth' (12:10, emphasis added). It is not a book of despair. The book's own conclusion calls itself a curriculum on *truth and delight.*

We do not need a book of the Bible to tell us that life is full of vanities.

Introduction

That is universally obvious in all human experience. What we do need, however, is instruction to know peace and joy in spite of such heartaches. That, I will argue in the present volume, is the message of Ecclesiastes.

It is also noteworthy that Ecclesiastes expresses a special concern for young people. At the culmination of the book, the writer offers this closing appeal to his audience: 'Rejoice, O young man, in your youth, and let your heart cheer you in the days of your youth' (11:9). Ecclesiastes calls especially to the youth in his audience, those standing on the brink of adulthood in an uncertain world, to embrace the lessons on joy here taught. Ecclesiastes is written so that all God's people, and especially young people, can embark on a life of godly joy despite the senseless uncertainties which lie ahead.

If we understand these things, it is hard to think of a more timely book for the presently emerging generation than Ecclesiastes. Bold technological advances in the twentieth century gave those generations hope that the world was improving. Today, we doubt the world is getting much better after all. Instead of providing hope for improvement, technology is more often used as an escape. It is precisely for such a time as this that Ecclesiastes faces the music, admits it is a dirge, yet teaches us a melody of joy.

Notes

1 Gordis, *Koheleth*, p. 39.

2 See Addison G. Wright, 'The Riddle of the Sphinx: The Structure of the Book of Qohelet', *Catholic Biblical Quarterly* 30 (1968), pp. 313–334; 'The Riddle of the Sphinx Revisited: Numerical Patterns in the Book of Qohelet', *Catholic Biblical Quarterly* 42 (1980), pp. 38–51.

3 Norman Whybray, 'Qoheleth, Preacher of Joy', *Journal for the Study of the Old Testament* 23 (1982), pp. 87–98.

Prologue: the guide, the map and the quest (1:1–18)

E very expedition needs a guide, a map, and a quest to accomplish. The prologue of Ecclesiastes (contained in the first chapter) introduces the book's guide, its map or outline, and the quest before us.

Our *guide* is 'the Preacher, the son of David, king in Jerusalem' (v. 1), whose peculiar title ('the Preacher') we will examine shortly. The *map* is a two-part course of study outlined at the close of the chapter (vv. 12–18). The *quest* of the book—to make sense of life's vanities—is also introduced in this chapter (vv. 2–11). In the next few pages, let's take stock of the guide, the quest and the map Ecclesiastes sets before us for this course on abiding joy.

Our guide (1:1)

The author of this book and our guide in this study is identified as Israel's most famous wise man, King Solomon (cf. 1:12, 16; 12:9). Today, scholars debate whether Solomon actually wrote the book, or if another wrote it using his name. There is no conclusive reason to dismiss the Solomonic ascription identifying this book as either composed by Solomon himself or composed under his oversight by sages in his court. Those interested in the question of authorship can consult other commentaries.[1] Here I want to focus on the peculiar title used for Solomon in the Ecclesiastes prologue. He is called 'the Preacher'.

In Hebrew, the word is *qohelet*. The word *qohelet* is often translated 'preacher' in English (*ecclesiastes* in Latin), but we should not think of a preacher in church when we read the title here. *Qohelet* literally means 'an assembler'. It is probably one of the titles of Israel's kings, in this case ascribed to Solomon as king. One of the king's duties in Israel was to assemble the people for instruction in times of turmoil.

We find a helpful example of such an assembly in the biblical account of Nehemiah. (Nehemiah was not a king, but he fulfilled many kingly duties.) There was an economic crisis in Nehemiah's day, and it was his duty as ruler to devise a solution. Nehemiah reports, 'I took counsel with myself, and [then] … I held a great assembly [*qehilah*[2]]' (Neh. 5:7). In that assembly, Nehemiah introduced his solution and persuaded all the key leaders to adopt his plan. That is the work of the ruler as the people's 'assembler' (*qohelet*).

Actually, our civic leaders fulfil this same duty today as well. When there is a national crisis in America, for example, the President gives a televised broadcast from the Oval Office. The purpose of that address is not to issue new laws: it is to explain the facts, describe the President's plan to meet the crisis, and to rally the people in support of what he believes will be the right way forward. Whenever the President does this, he is acting as the nation's 'assembler-in-chief'.

It is in this role that Solomon is introduced in the opening line of Ecclesiastes. He is not speaking to us as a lawgiver introducing new legislation. He speaks to us as the *qohelet* who assembles us in the face of a social crisis.

But the crisis to be addressed in this gathering is timeless. It is not a period economic collapse as in the days of Nehemiah. This assembly is to address the timeless problem of life's vanity. The Solomonic guidance in this book is also timeless, and it has been written down for the guidance of God's people in every generation.

In fact, there is a new son of David who now takes up the royal posts of God's anointed king. Jesus is identified in the New Testament as the new Son of David who inherits the duties of Assembler, First Judge, Chief Prophet, Psalmist,[3] and the other responsibilities of Israel's kings. Just as each of Israel's kings was to uphold the received books of the Hebrew canon (see Deut. 17:18–19; Prov. 25:1), it is King Jesus who has finally reappointed Ecclesiastes and the other books of Israel for our instruction (Luke 24:27, 44). Christ is the new King, Teacher and *Qohelet* who assembles us to heed these words of guidance. Ultimately, Jesus is 'the Preacher, the son of David' who speaks to us in Ecclesiastes.

Throughout this study, we will use the title 'Qohelet' to refer to the guide instructing us in this book. By using this title, we recognize both that Solomon is introduced as the original author of these words, and that Jesus is the Assembler who now affirms its conclusions to us.

If you trust Jesus, you can trust the agenda in this book to help you navigate life's vanities and find joy. But what is this 'vanity' that hinders proper joy?

The quest (1:2–11)

In this poem, Qohelet defines the problem of 'vanity'—the problem to be faced in the rest of the book. What is the problem of vanity?

In English, the word 'vanity' has a broad range of meanings. Sometimes we use the word to refer to pride. At its root, however, the word refers to something that is 'empty' or 'worthless'. A proud person is said to be 'vain' because his or her boasts of greatness are empty. The root meaning of the word 'vanity' in English is 'emptiness'.

The Hebrew word translated 'vanity' (*hebel*) also means 'empty'. Literally, *hebel* means 'like a vapour'. Something worthless is like a vapour. It has appearance but no substance. However, valuable things can also be 'like a vapour'. For example, in the first chapters of Genesis we are told how Cain killed his younger brother. That younger brother came to be remembered as Abel, or *Hebel* in Hebrew. His life was like a vapour, not because it lacked value but because it ended suddenly. Something of great value is also like vapour if it slips between your fingers and vanishes.

It is this aspect of life's vanity (its vapour-like uncertainty) that Qohelet captures in the poem at the heart of this chapter (vv. 2–11). Bear in mind that this is a poem that captures general truths succinctly. Critics will cast doubt upon the text by insisting that there are famous individuals who have been remembered long after their deaths (contrary to v. 11), and that there have been many new inventions especially in recent centuries (contrary to v. 10). Solomon would not have been blind to the memories of famous people or the progress of lasting achievements (even his own—e.g. 2 Chr. 2:1–5:1). Notwithstanding such accomplishments, however, the overwhelming vapidity of human life remains a problem to be faced. The vast majority of members of the human race live and die with no remembrance, and even the famous are eventually forgotten, dishonoured or caricatured in ways barely resembling reality. In ancient Egypt, pharaohs built massive pyramids and filled the land with statues and carved likenesses of themselves in order to keep their memories alive for ever—efforts that have essentially failed.

Likewise, though the modern world has enjoyed particularly impressive strides in technology, the human condition remains essentially unchanged. Life is extremely valuable, but it quickly ends, with little real impact on the world's persistent sorrows. It is the vapour-like impermanence of human efforts that this opening poem captures so eloquently.

But does this unavoidable impermanence of life and labour mean that all human effort is meaningless? No! Nowhere in this poem does Qohelet regard life as meaningless. This is a crucial insight for our study. The world is a wonderful place to live in, and life is full of beauty. In fact, it is only because life *does* have value and because human efforts *are* of great worth that this fact of impermanence is such a tragedy! Qohelet is not a nihilist; he is a realist.

Thus, the problem our Assembler (*qohelet*) has called us together to address is the problem of life's vanity (*hebel*). Our labours accomplish nothing lasting. And for all our efforts to understand, life's twists and turns continue to befuddle us. How are we to live in such a world? What are we to do with our lives in a world where nothing lasts and all is *hebel*?

The map (1:12–18)

In the final verses of the prologue, Qohelet gives us a 'table of contents' (or map) for the rest of the book. These paragraphs introduce the two-part course on which Qohelet will lead us. Notice the pattern in these two paragraphs. Each paragraph begins with an announcement of the writer's credentials (vv. 12, 16), follows with a statement of the problem he has studied ('I applied my heart to ...', vv. 13, 17), then concludes with a proverb (vv. 15, 18). This pattern breaks this closing section into two paragraphs, each raising a different frontier of life's vanity that will be explored in the two halves of the book that follow.

First (vv. 12–15), Qohelet promises to face the vanities of *human labour*: 'I applied my heart to seek and to search out by wisdom all that is done under heaven' (v. 13). His conclusion is frank: 'It is an unhappy business ... I have seen everything that is done under the sun, and behold, all is vanity and a striving after wind' (vv. 13–14). There will be no whitewashing of the problem here. Everything we do in life is plagued by vanity, and Qohelet will not ignore that reality.

The proverb that sums up this topic focuses on labour's limits: 'What is crooked cannot be made straight, and what is missing cannot be filled in' (v. 15, author's translation [a.t.]).[4] Straighten something, and there is always more to be straightened. Fill in what is lacking in one place, and there will always be another gap to fill. No system of labour is perfect and no job is lasting. This paragraph about the vanity of human labour is a teaser for the series of explorations ahead in the first half of Ecclesiastes (2:1–6:9), where Qohelet will explore the fleetingness of human toil.

In the second paragraph (vv. 16–18), Qohelet removes his worksite hard hat and dons his philosopher's cap. This paragraph takes up the enigmas of *human understanding*: 'I said in my heart, "I have acquired great wisdom …" And I applied my heart to know wisdom and to know madness and folly. I perceived that this also is but a striving after wind' (vv. 16–17).

We will not find naive platitudes here. There are intractable problems beyond human capacity to resolve. In fact, rather than satisfying, the quest for wisdom tends to 'increase sorrow' (v. 18). As one commentator explains, 'Open eyes see the injustices of society, and wider awareness of oppression and life's absurdities is disquieting.'[5] On its own, the quest for wisdom brings greater sorrow, not greater joy. This does not mean that wisdom is worthless or bad; there is a wisdom that brings joy. But it is the point of Qohelet to bring us to that joyful wisdom by first facing the reality of our inability to understand the world around us. In the second half of Ecclesiastes (6:10–12:7), Qohelet will lead us through the enigmas of *human understanding*.

You might be wondering how Ecclesiastes can be a book about joy (as I explained in the Preface) when it opens with such a dismal prologue. There is no promise of joy anywhere in Ecclesiastes 1, only a thorough admission of life's vanities. In fact, the final verse of the chapter is one that speaks of the increasing *sorrow* of those who pursue understanding.

Such a prologue shows us the pastoral heart of the book's author. Qohelet writes for real people with real sorrows in life. He writes, not simply for those who are curious to learn, but also for those who are overcome with real disillusionment.

Like a movie reviewer eager to explain why a certain film is a 'must see', I have already spoiled the plot. I have 'spilled the beans' by telling you up front that the book ultimately brings us to a robust lesson on joy. But the original writer does not spoil the plot in his opening prologue. He simply meets us where we live in life's troubles.

Ecclesiastes is a book that faces the music and admits it is a dirge. Later, the author will show us how the fear of the Lord gives us a melody powerful enough to fill our hearts with joy, even amid life's harshest vanities. But he first assures us he fully understands—and agrees—that life is fundamentally *hebel* (vain).

Notes

1 See Fredericks, 'Ecclesiastes', pp. 31–36.
2 *Qehilah* is an 'assembly', as called together by the *qohelet* (or the 'assembler').
3 On Jesus' role as the new Psalm leader of God's people, see Michael LeFebvre, *Singing the Songs of Jesus: Revisiting the Psalms* (Fearn: Christian Focus, 2010).
4 The ESV translates the closing line 'what is lacking cannot be counted'. I have accepted the argument of Michael Fox that the phrase should read, 'no deficiency can be filled out'. Fox, *A Time to Tear Down*, p. 170.
5 Crenshaw, *Ecclesiastes*, p. 76.

Part 1
Lessons on labour

In pursuit of pleasure: the vanity and value of labour's rewards (2:1–26)

When the automobile was first introduced, critics doubted that such a complex piece of machinery could replace the ancient relationship between a man and his horse. Early automobiles were prone to malfunction and were easily bogged down in mud in those days before paved roads. When a horseback rider spotted a broken-down car, he was apt to yell, 'Get a horse!'

Eventually, the kinks were worked out of those early designs. The automobile did emerge as a reliable technology, in most respects more practical for travel than a horse.

Unfortunately, the same cannot be said for the fragility of life's pleasures. Technology, like the automobile, can be improved, and profit can add convenience and pleasure to life. However, the persistent vanities of life do not go away, and the pleasure of labour's rewards is uncertain and shallow in the face of life's sorrows.

Does this mean the Christian ought to avoid the pursuit of reward altogether? Should the Christian cry, 'Get a horse!'—or in this case, 'Quit your job!'? No, but neither should God's people be sucked into the false allure of this-worldly pleasures. In the case of the automobile, early problems were resolved. In the case of life's unfairness and vagaries, however, there is no solution at hand.

In Qohelet's first lesson, he confronts the vanities of reward and teaches a more certain basis for joy in our labours.

Chapter 2

The study of pleasure (2:1–3)

Qohelet introduces his first lesson in verses 1–2: the vanity of those pleasures obtained by human labour. What a fitting place to start! The pursuit of pleasure is so basic to human experience that we should not be surprised to find its examination at the front of Qohelet's book.

Some think this chapter describes a hedonistic binge, as though King Solomon threw caution to the wind and went on a mindless pleasure spree. Perhaps our own sinful hearts lead us to imagine such indulgences in this chapter, but the text is clear that that is not the case. With phrases like 'my heart still guiding me with wisdom' (v. 3) and 'my wisdom remained with me' (v. 9), Qohelet emphasizes that his pleasures were always moderated.[1] It is a chapter about hard work to acquire the rewards for which people labour—and doing so prudently. This chapter examines the honest rewards of labour, not hedonism.

A further clarification is in order with regard to verse 3. The writer says that he sought by wisdom 'to lay hold on folly'. Many readers are puzzled at this use of the word 'folly'. How can Qohelet moderate his quest with wisdom, if his quest is 'to lay hold on folly'?

A simple distinction will help resolve this puzzle: Qohelet is not seeking to lay hold on *foolishness*, but on *things* that prove to be foolish pursuits. The 'follies' the writer seeks to lay hold on are the pleasurable rewards listed in the following verses: houses, musicians, and the like (vv. 4–8). These are not immoral, nor are they foolish in and of themselves. By calling them 'follies', Qohelet is anticipating the final result of his examination concerning their value as reasons for life.[2]

The final result of Qohelet's study will show that all such pleasures are frivolous. For this reason, he playfully calls his study 'a wise study of follies'. There is no contradiction here, only a poetic contrast that makes his conclusions clear from the start.

A catalogue of pleasures (2:4–11)

As Israel's king, Solomon developed a profitable network of businesses. Sometimes we mistakenly assume that ancient kings sat lazily on their thrones taxing the peasants. Perhaps some corrupt kings did fall into such behaviour, but proper kingship is about leadership. That includes the development of businesses in the land. Solomon worked hard to set up profitable enterprises in Israel (see 1 Kings 10:14–15, 28–29). And he succeeded, surpassing all the preceding rulers in Jerusalem (which included the many Jebusite kings in Jerusalem before David, v. 9). Through labour and business acumen (his wisdom), Solomon acquired all the pleasant rewards for which people work.

Ten categories of rewards are listed in verses 4–8. The first five are pleasures the king built: houses, vineyards, gardens and parks, orchards, and pools of water. The latter five are rewards he purchased or otherwise accumulated: slaves, herds and flocks, silver and gold, singers, and concubines (or 'sexual enjoyments'). These ten items represent the idyllic pleasures of kings. Today, we might compile a very different list of ideal pleasures. Our list might include stocks, cars and gadgets. This list represents the chief delights for which people laboured in Solomon's day.

Two of the items on this list introduce moral questions: slaves and concubines. Regarding the first, Old Testament law prohibited Israel owning other human beings like animals. What is called chattel slavery (owning people as one would own cattle) was not permitted in Israel. The form of slavery that did exist was debt slavery. This was not slavery as commonly understood today, but rather a prescribed period of indenture to work off debts. It is unlikely, therefore, that human trafficking is what Qohelet has in mind; rather it is the inexpensive (but humane) labour of indentured servants (see Excursus at the end of this chapter).

The final item on Qohelet's list of pleasures is often translated 'concubines'. This is, however, an imprecise translation. The Hebrew expression does indicate sexual abundance, but it does not state whether that fulfilment is with one or many partners. The other Solomonic wisdom books (Proverbs and Song of Songs) extol the place of sexual pleasure within marriage, and it is unnecessary to imagine that Ecclesiastes exalts a different ethic. In fact, later in Ecclesiastes we will encounter exhortations to sexual fidelity (7:23–29; 9:9). In light of the pervasive emphasis on sexual fidelity within the Solomonic wisdom books, it would be better to translate the last phrase on Qohelet's list of kingly pleasures 'sexual enjoyments', without imposing a promiscuous assumption not present in the Hebrew.[3]

Taken at face value, the list of kingly pleasures in this passage contains no sinful indulgences. It simply captures an ancient summary of idyllic comforts. At the close of the list, the writer acknowledges the enjoyment he found in his wealth. He enjoyed his gardens, flocks and music. 'My heart found pleasure in all my toil, and this was my reward for all my toil' (v. 10). The text does not downplay the pleasure brought by labour's income; but it ultimately concedes that all such rewards are incomplete and fleeting: 'all was vanity and a striving after wind' (v. 11). It is in the next segment that Qohelet explains this stunning conclusion.

Examining the results (2:12–23)

The vanity of profit is nowhere illustrated so clearly as in the custom of inheritance. This is the topic Qohelet introduces in verses 12–23 to demonstrate the inherent vanity of income. It is not the practice of leaving an inheritance that is the problem. Leaving an inheritance is a good thing (cf. Prov. 13:22). However, by focusing on the inherent inequity that emerges even within a good custom like leaving an inheritance, Qohelet is exposing the fundamental unfairness (vanity) that pervades the distribution of all labour's reward.

Qohelet introduces the main topic of inheritance in verse 12: 'Then I turned to consider wisdom and madness and folly, for what kind of man will come after me who will rule over what has already been done?'

(v. 12, a.t.).[4] It is not 'wisdom and madness and folly' as abstract virtues and vices that Qohelet considers; it is the nature of the man who will come after him—whether he will be one of wisdom, or of madness and folly—that the writer considers.[5]

There are actually two sides to the inequity revealed by the custom of inheritance. The first is described in verses 13–17. It is through wisdom that accomplishments are made. Twice the text emphasizes the 'gain' achieved by wisdom (v. 13). Wisdom (and not folly) brings reward in one's labours. Nevertheless, the ultimate reward at the end of every life is death. Whether one is wise or foolish, the same ultimate reward comes to all. This is the first inequity experienced in human inheritance. Based on this first problem, Qohelet concludes that life 'under the sun' (more on that phrase shortly) is grievous and hateful (v. 17).

Qohelet explains the second troubling upshot of his inheritance scenario in verses 18–23. His work 'under the sun' (which previously brought him pleasure, v. 10) is found to be hateful when he considers the inequity of its actual disposition. The wise generation sweats, bleeds, sacrifices and suffers. But if the heir is foolish, the wrong kind of person enjoys the pleasure. This is unfair. It is inequitable. It is an inherent vanity in life.[6]

This inheritance scenario is simply a teaching example. The passage is not presenting a thorough analysis of all the inequities of wealth to prove that rewards are plagued by vanity. This single scenario is meant to illustrate the point. It may not be through inheritance; the foolish may acquire the wealth of the wise through theft, unjust redistribution, a family feud, a foreclosure, or through many other means. Qohelet is offering one scenario to illustrate multifaceted realities. Rewards are pleasant, but they are never secure. And often they are distributed inequitably.

There are strong words at the heart of Qohelet's complaint about these vanities of wealth (vv. 17–18). Qohelet says that he 'hated' life in such a system of inequities, and he 'hated' all his works when he realized the absurdity of their ultimate distribution. This powerful language is the kind of expression that leads many readers to conclude that the book of Ecclesiastes is a book of despair. On the contrary, these strong words are used because the vanities of life 'under the sun' truly are hateful. Qohelet takes the naive enthusiasm which swells the heart as we imagine that earlier list of kingly delights, and he bursts the bubble with the 'hatred' of those very pleasures once the true absurdity of life 'under the sun' is considered. But this honest hatefulness of the broken order of life 'under the sun' is not the end of the matter.

I have quoted the phrase 'under the sun' several times. Qohelet states it numerous times in this passage, including once with each of his remarks about the hatefulness of life (v. 17) and of toil (v. 18). This phrase 'under the sun' is used twenty-nine times in the book of Ecclesiastes.[7] Its meaning can be best appreciated by contrasting it with another, similar expression often found in Scripture: the phrase 'under the heavens'.

Choon-Leon Seow explains, 'Whereas "under the heavens" is a spatial designation (referring to what is happening in the world), the expression "under the sun" is temporal, referring to the experiences in the realm of the living.'[8] In other words, the phrase refers to the order of present day-by-day experience: life under the rising and setting of the sun. Within the present order of human experience (life 'under the sun'), the inequities of labour are a source of despair. But life 'under the sun' is not the perspective in which we are to live. We experience the vanities of life 'under the sun', and Qohelet does not promise us any ways to solve those inequities. Nevertheless, the writer is divorcing us from the illusions of pleasure, not to leave us in 'under the sun' despair, but to teach us a more solid foundation for joy.

Call to joy (2:24–26)
In the chapter's final paragraph, we are led out of the gloom of life's

vanities into the shimmering promise of joy at God's hand. 'There is nothing better for a person than that he should eat and drink and find enjoyment in his toil. This also, I saw, is from the hand of God' (v. 24). There is joy to be had in our labours—and in the rewards of our labours (i.e. eating and drinking). But joy comes from God's pleasure in us as we toil, not from the illusive pleasures of wealth. 'For to the one who pleases him God has given … joy' (v. 26).

There is a striking promise in the closing verse of the chapter (v. 26). Qohelet assures us that God is the one who gives joy to his people now, *and* he is the one who determines the final distribution of the rewards of human labours later. The one who worships God (i.e. 'the one who pleases him') is blessed with 'wisdom and knowledge and joy'. Meanwhile, 'the sinner' (i.e. the one who is not right with God) is busy 'gathering and collecting' the kinds of pleasures just described in this chapter. However, the ultimate disposition of the labours of the sinner is to be, under the hand of God, for the benefit of his own people.

Qohelet's words reflect the promise elsewhere in Scripture that 'the meek shall inherit the earth' (Ps. 37:11; Matt. 5:5; cf. Isa. 65:17; 2 Peter 3:13). The Canaanites prospered in their land for a time; but because of their sins, the houses and farms they built in the Promised Land were ultimately brought into the heritage of those who lived in gratefulness and obedience to God (Gen. 15:16; Exod. 23:29–31). God is the one who grants wisdom and joy to his people and who will bring the world to final judgement. In the final line, it is the 'gathering and collecting' of the sinner that receives the ultimate designation 'vanity and a striving after wind' (v. 26).

Rather than seeking pleasure, Qohelet teaches us to enjoy labour and its rewards (however limited or inequitable) in the service of God. Note the relational language he uses: 'This also, I saw, is *from the hand* of God, *for apart from him* who can … have enjoyment?' (vv. 24–25, emphasis added; cf. 1 Cor. 10:31). Rather than seeking pleasure in work's rewards,

Qohelet calls us to discover the joy of work done in communion with God and of rewards enjoyed in his service. The inevitable inequities we will suffer cannot spoil that joy, for God is the one who makes every injustice right in the end.

Excursus: slaves in Ecclesiastes 2:7

The Bible's position on slavery has long been a subject of controversy. Sadly, the Scriptures have sometimes been misused to endorse the buying and selling of people as human cattle. This treatment of people as property is called 'chattel slavery'. A careful reading of the Old Testament law reveals that Israel was *not* permitted to engage in *chattel* slavery. In fact, the Old Testament law was radically different from the laws of other ancient societies because of the humane treatment (e.g. Lev. 25:43; Deut. 23:15–16), protections (e.g. Exod. 21:26–27), limitations of service (e.g. Deut. 15:12) and even generosity (e.g. Deut. 15:13–15, 18) required for unpaid labourers.

The 'slavery' of the Old Testament was not chattel slavery like that of nineteenth-century Europe and America. Israel had experienced such slavery in Egypt, and the Mosaic law forbade such a system in Israel (e.g. Exod. 21:16; Lev. 19:34; 25:42; Deut. 15:15). The labour called 'slavery' in Israel was so called because it was unpaid or obligatory, not because the labourers were considered or treated as subhuman (cf. Job 31:13–15).

In some cases, kings undertaking great building projects would draft the labour of foreigners living in the land (e.g. 1 Kings 9:15–23). This was forced labour (a draft). But it was not racial slavery (prohibited in Lev. 19:34), nor turning people into property (prohibited in Exod. 21:16). Foreigners living in the land were those who were not already part of a household farm or business. Those not attached to landed families would serve as day-workers in odd jobs on a day-by-day basis (e.g. Matt. 20:1–16). A royal draft was a command summons of all such workers not attached to household businesses to serve in labour projects for the king.

This was forced labour, because it was obligatory; but these corvée labourers retained their full legal rights (e.g. 2 Sam. 21:1–14). Furthermore, they were treated as humans and not as cattle. It was not chattel slavery; it was a labour draft.

In other cases, slavery was a way in which indebted individuals worked off their debts (e.g. Exod. 21:1–6; Lev. 25:39–41; Deut. 15:7–15; Neh. 5:4–5). There was no debtors prison in Israel. When a debtor defaulted on a loan, he would fulfil the debt obligation by working without pay for the creditor or by being 'sold' for the value of the loan to work in another household for the duration required to satisfy the debt. The individuals so bound retained their own private property, and they were not themselves human property. They were, in some respects, like sons and daughters added to the family (e.g. Lev. 22:10–11), working for their lodging without pay as the children of the house did, but without inheritance rights. (However, a slave who served well might be written into the inheritance by an appreciative master; see Prov. 17:2; Ezek. 46:16–18.)

Such debt slavery was temporary, and it ended once the value of the debt had been recouped through labour. Furthermore, no debt slavery could last longer than six years no matter how great the debt (e.g. Exod. 21:2; Deut. 15:12). The permanent attachment of a debt slave to a household was prohibited, with three exceptions: a female servant who married into the household where she served would become a permanent part of the house, and she was to be treated as a full daughter of the household (Exod. 21:7–11); a male servant who married another debt slave or member of the household (so that his children were members of that household, like sons of the family, albeit without inheritance rights, Exod. 21:4) could become a permanent part of the household if he desired (Exod. 21:5–6); and, if a debt slave found his food, lodging and care in the present household better than his prospects on his own and so desired to remain, he could do so (Deut. 15:16–17). Thus, careful protections were put in place to guard debt slavery in Israel from ever turning into chattel slavery. Furthermore, the discipline described for slaves in the Bible is actually the same discipline which was administered to sons. As in the case of discipline for sons, the discipline of debt slaves had to be administered without anger or abuse (cf. Exod. 21:20–21; Prov. 13:24). Such household 'debt slaves' in Israel were not, therefore, chattel slaves. Perhaps they should be called 'bondservants' or 'indentured servants' instead of 'slaves' to make the distinction clear.

The only passages in the Old Testament where slaves are called 'property' are Leviticus 22:11 and 25:44–46. These two instances where the label 'property' (*ahuzzah*) is attached to slaves do not, however, mean that household slaves were regarded as subhuman or chattel slaves. The term simply distinguishes those participants in the household who were acquired through inheritance or an economic transaction from those born into the household. There were members of the household who had inheritance rights, and there were members of the household who 'were inherited' as part of the family estate. The term 'property' simply identifies those who were part of the latter category.

Boaz, for example, 'bought' (*qanah*) Ruth as part of an inheritance redemption (Ruth 4:5). Ruth became part of the inheritance of Boaz's household through his purchase, and then he married her. Scripture even identifies God as property (*ahuzzah*) inherited by the Levites. Each of the tribes of Israel inherited land as their property, except the Levites, for whom God was their inherited property (Ezek. 44:28). The Levites were similarly identified as 'a gift' to the priests (Num. 18:6). There is nothing dehumanizing about these terms of possession as used in the aforementioned references. In fact, the term 'property' (*ahuzzah*) used of household slaves in Leviticus 22:11 was meant to show the greater (not lesser) rights of slaves who were attached to the family inheritance in contrast with hired servants. Those who were attached to the household estate (those who were 'property', *'ahuzzah* of the priests) were permitted to eat the holy food. Hired servants were not.

The other passage where slaves are called 'property' (Lev. 25:44–46) is part of the laws about the Jubilee Festival. It is not a chapter setting up additional laws or exceptions about slavery; it is a chapter about the Jubilee Festival, where this provision identifies those household slaves who were to be freed as part of the celebration and those who were not. All circumcised slaves (that is, all worshippers of Yahweh) were to be freed as part of the celebration of God's liberty. Only non-circumcised slaves—specifically those acquired by economic transactions as household 'property' (*'ahuzzah*)—were to continue as part of the family heritage. Slaves who were born into the household would be circumcised (Gen. 17:12–13). Also, foreign slaves who converted to the faith of Israel would also have been circumcised and would have participated in all the Hebrew festivals, including Jubilees (Exod. 12:44).

When English-speaking readers see the term 'property' ascribed to slaves in those two passages (Lev. 22:11; 25:44–46), it is common for them to mistake that label as contradicting what we have seen about slavery in the rest of the Old Testament. However, the Scriptures repeatedly point to Israel's experience of slavery in Egypt as something never to be imposed by Israel upon others. The Old Testament law prohibited treating human beings as objects (esp. Exod. 21:16; Lev. 19:34), and biblical references to slavery should not be read in light of pre-Civil War American chattel slavery and its abuses.

The purpose of this review of slavery in the Old Testament is to explain Solomon's reference to slaves in the list of labour's rewards in Ecclesiastes 2:7. When the passage is read within the context of Hebrew law and culture, we ought to conclude that the 'slaves' in Ecclesiastes 2:7 were not chattel slaves. Scripture tells us that Solomon drafted forced labour teams (1 Kings 9:15–23). He may also have had many debt slaves working on his estates. These are the kinds of slaves which the Old Testament

Scriptures permitted in Israel and which are mentioned in Ecclesiastes. Terms like 'draft labour' and 'debt slaves' would be more helpful than 'slaves' in order to avoid the inaccurate perception that the Israelites owned slaves in the same (and immoral) way as pre-Civil War America and pre-Exodus Egypt.

Notes

1 There is an important word play in v. 3 that is hard to see in most English translations. The verse reads, 'I searched with my heart how to draw [*limesok*] my body with wine, my heart yet leading [*noheg*] in wisdom' (v. 3, a.t.). That unusual expression 'how to draw (or pull) my body with wine' is usually translated 'how to cheer my body with wine'. That is undoubtedly the right idea: Qohelet is enjoying his wine. But he uses the verb 'draw' for the effect of wine on the body in order to follow with the complementary verb 'lead' for the overall control of wisdom in his heart. The result is an expression that is awkward to translate into English, but which is striking in its meaning. The writer wants to be clear that his enjoyment of life's pleasures was governed by prudence.

2 Fox, *A Time to Tear Down*, p. 179.

3 A more precise translation is possible, but the literal translation is uncomfortable for modern readers. The original Hebrew uses *shiddah weshiddot*, a syntactically intensified plural form of the word for 'breast'. Both Proverbs and Song of Songs likewise use physical references to express the sexual activity between marriage partners (e.g. Prov. 5:19; S. of S. 1:13). Of course, Solomon himself had many wives and concubines, but the Scriptures always condemn this aspect of his life (e.g. 1 Kings 11:3). The roundabout expression used for sexual fulfilment in Eccles. 2:8 (i.e. without referring to numerous partners) is probably a deliberate effort to avoid condoning the way Solomon experienced this pleasure.

4 My translation of v. 12 is different from that in most English Bibles. Most translations render it in a manner like the following: 'So I turned to consider wisdom and madness and folly. For what can the man do who comes after the king? Only what has already been done' (ESV). However, other translators recognize the contextual and linguistic factors leading to translations like my own. For instance, HCSB has: 'Then I turned to consider wisdom, madness, and folly, for what will the man be like who comes after the king? He will do what has already been done.' See also, especially, the translation and arguments of Michael Fox: 'And I turned to observe wisdom and inanity and folly, for what will the man be like who will come after me, who will rule over what I earned earlier?' Fox, *A Time to Tear Down*, p. 181.

5 Fox, *A Time to Tear Down*, pp. 181–183.

6 The story of Solomon and his son Rehoboam (1 Kings 12:1–15) reveals that Solomon's fears were justified. Rehoboam was foolish, and he squandered all that his father had laboured hard to build. Such examples of the fool benefiting from the labours of the wise are too common in human society.

7 Eccles. 1:3, 9, 14; 2:11, 17–20 (x 4), 22; 3:16; 4:1, 3, 7, 15; 5:13, 18; 6:1, 12; 8:9, 15 (x 2), 17; 9:3, 6, 9 (x 2), 11, 13; 10:5.

8 Choon-Leon Seow, *Ecclesiastes: A New Translation with Introduction* (AB 18C; New York: Doubleday, 1997), p. 113. It has been common to interpret 'under the sun' as a spatial expression, as though the writer is dividing the place of God ('above the sun') from the place of men ('under the sun'; e.g. Matthew Henry, *Commentary on the Whole Bible* (6 vols; New York: Fleming H. Revell, 1935), vol. 3, p. 982). Whether the term is meant to divide (spatially) the place of God and men, or (temporally) the world as now experienced from the world as it ought to be, the theological implication is essentially the same: 'under the sun' marks off the realm of present human life from that of ideal, divine correction.

Children of the age: the uncertainty of labour's seasons (3:1–15)

When we want to be entertained or inspired, we turn to artists. When we want to understand, we turn to scientists. That, at least, is the common disposition of our age. But art has instructional value too. A painting, a movie, a song or a poem can offer insights into 'how things work' as aptly as any scientific lecture—sometimes more effectively.

In the next section of Ecclesiastes, Qohelet dons his poet's hat and recites a poem (vv. 1–8). Then he leads us in an analysis of the truth it teaches us (vv. 9–15). This is not a luncheon of the local poetry club, however. This is the next instalment in our Assembler's education on 'how the world works' and the way to true joy despite its uncertainties.

A poem on seasons (3:1–8)

Like a scientific paper, this poem opens with a thesis statement: 'For everything there is a season, and a time for every matter under heaven' (v. 1). The rest of the poem lays out examples that illustrate this principle and demonstrate that it is true.

There is an elegant cadence to the poem. Each line presents a contrast, swaying between positive and negative poles. Some lines start with a positive image and end with its negative counterpart (e.g. born → die; plant → pluck up; seek → lose). Other lines switch the cadence the other way, beginning on a sad note and ending with the happy idea (e.g. kill → heal; break down → build up; weep → laugh). The result is a balanced rhythm that communicates both sides of every contrast, yet the overall poem both begins and ends on a positive footing. The first line begins positively ('a time to be born', v. 2a) and the last line ends positively ('a time for peace', v. 8b). In other words, even though the poem gives equal time to the positive and to the negative events of life, it gives favoured positions to the joyful seasons of life. Even in the subtle shaping of this poem, there is reason to believe that Ecclesiastes comes to us from a teacher of joy, not of sorrow.

It is also important to notice the number of contrasts contained in this lyric. There are fourteen examples (vv. 2–8). In Hebrew, the number seven represents completeness. As a poem with fourteen contrasts (seven doubled), Qohelet's masterpiece conveys a strong sense of comprehensiveness. Undoubtedly, he could have included many more examples, but the poem is manageably brief. Nevertheless, by choosing fourteen examples, Qohelet assures us that these specimens illustrate a universal principle: 'For *everything* there is a season, and a time for *every matter* under heaven' (v. 1, emphasis added).

Let's look more closely at two of the contrasts in this poem. First, let's look at verse 2: '[There is] a time to be born, and a time to die.'

Abraham Lincoln was born on 12 February 1809, and he died at the hands of an assassin on 15 April 1865. Were those precise dates predestined as Lincoln's 'time to be born' and 'time to die'? According to other passages in the Bible, God does sovereignly govern the very days and dates of our lives (e.g. Ps. 139:16). However, date-setting is not the point of this verse in Ecclesiastes. In this verse, Qohelet refers to the right *timing* (not the specific dates) for birth and death to occur.

The Hebrew word 'time' (*et*) used in this verse and throughout this poem does not usually refer to dates. There is a different Hebrew word that is used when an appointed time—that is, a specific date—is in view (*zeman*).[1] But the word featured in this poem (*et*) refers to seasons or conditions.[2] To say, for instance, that there is 'a time for war' (v. 8) does not mean that a calendar date exists on which attacks are scheduled, but that there are certain political and practical conditions conducive to war.

When Qohelet says there is 'a time to be born', then, he is not talking about birth dates; he is affirming that there are conditions that indicate that the moment for birth has arrived. As a baby forms in the womb, there comes a window of time during which birth is proper. A baby ought to be born at around forty weeks' gestation. When a child is born significantly earlier than that, the child is said to have been born 'prematurely'.[3] There is a time when birth is proper.

Similarly, there is a time when death is natural. Death is always tragic. There is never a 'right' time for death. But there is a stage in human ageing when death is fitting, and loved ones are able to say, 'He lived a full life.' When someone dies before that stage, whether through a sudden tragedy or a terminal disease, we often say that the person died 'before his time' (cf. 7:17; Ps. 90:10). In this sense, Abraham Lincoln died before his time, being shot shortly after his fifty-sixth birthday.

Let's look at a second example—or pair of examples—in verse 4: '[There is] a time to weep, and a time to laugh; a time to mourn, and a time to dance.' These two contrasts go together. The first set contrasts the basic, individual *acts* of joy and sorrow: weeping and laughing. The second contrasts the *rites* or *customs* observed as groups share in joy or sorrow together: the word 'mourn' in this usage probably refers to the rites of mourning, and the word for 'dance' likely has in mind a celebratory event, not just 'moving to music'. Here are opposite individual and corporate acts of joy and sorrow. Each has its time.

Suppose a relative of yours got engaged and your entire extended family gathered that summer for the wedding. That gathering would be 'a time to laugh' (there would be joy) and 'a time to dance' (there would be a reception). Now, to continue the illustration, suppose a beloved grandparent died the following year. Your extended family would gather again the next summer. But this time, it would be 'a time to weep' (there would be grieving) and 'a time to mourn' (there would be a funeral service). The exact same people would gather two summers in a row, but there would be a very different 'time' that determined the nature of each gathering.

These contrasts—and the other contrasts in the poem—further confirm Qohelet's point. There are conditions in life that determine what it is fitting to do or what we can expect to take place. This is not a passage about situational ethics. The text never contrasts moral and immoral actions, as though 'there is a time to give, and there is a time to steal'. None of the terms in this list describe immoral deeds.

The most troubling contrast is in verse 3: '[there is] a time to kill, and a time to heal.' But the fact that 'healing' is the contrast to 'kill' in this passage indicates that the setting is likely agrarian rather than judicial (or criminal!) killing. That is, the reference is not to killing other people but to a farmer's handling injured livestock. There are circumstances that indicate that an injured sheep or cow should be treated and healed. But there are circumstances when an illness or injury requires that the animal be 'put down'. There are passages in the Bible that provide instruction regarding judicial execution (e.g. Gen. 9:6; Exod. 21:12), but Ecclesiastes 3:4 is not one of them.

Each of the fourteen contrasts captures such opposite actions (but never immoral actions), admitting that a person's circumstances dictate which is correct. The poem in verses 1–8 establishes this universal principle about the seasons of life. It is a principle that is still relevant today.

In the next paragraph (vv. 9–11), Qohelet teaches us the implications of this fact of life.

The lesson of life's seasons (3:9–11)

The question at the head of verse 9 wraps up the humbling lesson of Qohelet's poem about seasons. 'What gain has the worker from his toil?' It is not really our own toil that determines our fruitfulness, but the season in which we labour. Two farmers might plant seed, each in his own field. The labour of each farmer is essential for the seed to grow, but it is the rain or lack thereof that determines the outcome of their labours. If one farm goes through a drought while the other experiences an ideal growing season, their outcomes will be very different. Qohelet's question in verse 9 calls us to re-examine our assumption that our own labours are to credit for our fruitfulness in life.

Qohelet gives us two doctrines (or teachings) about our labours that we need to understand. Having examined all the work God has appointed to humanity, Qohelet distils these two doctrines for us about the seasons of our labour.

First, God is the one who 'has made everything beautiful in its time' (v. 11). It is not mere attractiveness that is in view here. Something is beautiful when it is properly proportioned and complete, having attained its intended ideal. Qohelet is talking about the fact that God is the one who brings our labours to completion. He probably uses the word 'beautiful' (*yapeh*) rather than a more mundane term of completion (e.g. 'complete', *kalah*) because of the satisfaction and delight it expresses. We must do the appropriate work belonging to the seasons in which we find ourselves, yet it is God who brings about the beauty of each task in its season. That is the first doctrine Qohelet teaches us.

A second teaching about the seasons of our labour is expressed in these words: 'Also, he has put eternity into man's heart, yet so that he cannot find out what God has done from the beginning to the end' (v. 11b). The human heart longs to understand 'the big picture'. We yearn to see the ultimate, 'beautiful' outcome of our labours. This longing is what is meant by the phrase 'he has put eternity into man's heart'.[4] Let me illustrate this second doctrine about our yearning for eternity.

Construction on Notre Dame Cathedral in Paris began in the year 1163. According to legend, the bishop of Paris, Maurice de Sully, had a vision in which he saw the completed cathedral and sketched it on the ground. Over the following two centuries, several generations of architects and building crews laboured on the project. In 1345, the cathedral was finally finished.

Not a single person working on Notre Dame saw the entire project. Everyone who took part in its construction was constrained by the limits of his or her time. Yet undoubtedly, many of them laboured with an eager (albeit impossible) wish to have seen that original moment when Bishop Sully launched the work, and to see that final moment when the building would be done. The multi-generational construction of Notre Dame illustrates what Qohelet teaches about all of life. All of life is one grand project in the hands of God. He is the one who sovereignly governs the entire process, bringing each task to beauty in its season. He also is the only one who superintends the project from beginning to end. Nevertheless, in spite of our limitations, God has given us a desire to see the whole.

We long to see beyond the horizons of our own seasons to the ultimate outcome of things. But why would God create us with hearts that yearn for something he also leaves us incapable of attaining? Isn't it cruel to give people a hunger which they are constrained from satisfying? If God were merely taunting us, it would indeed be cruel. But Qohelet sees it differently, because God has a rich and meaningful reason for ordering life in this manner.

Call to joy (3:12–15)

We are given two responses to the doctrines discussed above. Each response is introduced by the phrase 'I perceived that …', first in verse 12 and repeated in verse 14.

First we read, 'I perceived that there is nothing better for them than to be joyful and to do good as long as they live; also that everyone should eat and drink and take pleasure in all his toil—this is God's gift to man' (vv. 12–13). This first instruction seems to answer the first doctrine taught earlier. Because God is the one who makes all things beautiful in their proper seasons (the first doctrine about seasons, v. 11a), we are free to rejoice in our labours, whatever fruits our own seasons may bring. The rewards we experience, however great or small, are God's gift and are not to be regarded as our own achievement.

Second, we read, 'I perceived that whatever God does endures for ever; nothing can be added to it, nor anything taken from it. God has done it, so that people fear before him' (v. 14). The first sentence restates the finding in verse 11b, namely that God puts the yearning for eternity in our hearts but reserves to himself the power of enduring results. We can never frustrate his purposes. The first sentence of this verse sums up what we have learned already, but now Qohelet adds an explanation why. 'God has done it, so that people fear before him' (v. 14).

Here is the great purpose statement behind all the limitations placed upon us by the seasons in which we labour. God has not ordained life this way to frustrate us, but rather to compel us to work in communion with himself!

This is the first time the expression 'fear God' appears in Ecclesiastes ('fear before him' in this instance). It will not be the last time we see this phrase. The fear of the Lord is a theme we will encounter many more times in this book (esp. 5:7; 7:18; 8:12–13; 12:13). In fact, 'fearing the Lord' is the centrepiece of Qohelet's conclusion for the entire book (12:13–14). It is no overstatement to say that fearing God is the key this book offers us for knowing robust joy in a world of uncertainties. One purpose of this section on seasons has been to introduce us to the fear of the Lord.

Let's take a moment to think about this phrase 'the fear of the Lord'. The Hebrew word 'fear' (*yare´*) means more than just 'being scared'. To get a handle on what it means to fear God, let's first consider an English word with an analogous range of meaning: *passion*.

The English word *passion* can refer to intense suffering, intense hatred or intense love. When we speak about the passion of Christ, we are talking about his suffering as he went to the cross. When we speak of two lovers and their passion for one another, we refer to their overwhelming love. The word can also be used for hatred, as in 'to hate with a passion'. According to Dictionary.com, *passion* is 'any powerful or compelling emotion or feeling, as love or hate'. The key word there is 'compelling'; passion denotes the all-consuming character of the love, hatred or suffering in view.

The Hebrew word *yare'* (fear) has a similar breadth including both all-consuming love and hatred. Fear is, after all, the most powerful human emotion. Fear is the emotion that cannot be ignored. It cannot be set aside even temporarily. Fear always commands front and centre attention in our hearts. When fear is experienced, all other priorities take second place to that which commands our fear.

It is in this sense that Scripture teaches us to fear God. We are not being taught to cower before him like terrified children before an unpredictable, abusive father. God's enemies ought to run from his wrath in terror, but his beloved children bow in fear (*yare'*) that is marked by awe-inspired love, not dread terror. In English, we do not use the word 'fear' that way. But in Hebrew, to fear God is to love him with that reverent awe which captivates one's whole heart, soul, mind and strength.

In Ecclesiastes 3:14 Qohelet tells us that God gives us hearts for eternity but limits us to our seasons for this reason: so that we might learn to fear him. There is nothing better than to do what is good in the seasons through which God leads us, trusting him to make everything beautiful in its proper time. It is only in this faith that we are able truly to eat and drink with joy (vv. 12–13).

The closing verse—'That which is, already has been; that which is to be, already has been; and God seeks what has been driven away' (v. 15)— is a fascinating conclusion to this passage. However, a different translation is needed. Most commentators admit that the Hebrew behind this verse is difficult to understand, and the awkwardness of its translation in various English Bibles shows it.

The verb often translated 'seek' in this verse (*baqash*) can convey the connotation of one's 'desire'. Furthermore, the verb translated 'what has been driven away' (*radap*) literally means, 'what has been pursued'. Accordingly, the verse could be translated, 'That which is, has already been; that which is to be, has already been; for God desires [of us] what has already been pursued.' In other words, it is God's design that each generation should labour in the same pursuits as previous generations.[5]

Translated this way, the final verse of the passage succinctly sums up what we have learned and adds an important closing assertion. The limitations placed upon us by life's repetitive and uncertain seasons are not due to the world's brokenness. The aspect of life's uncertainty that we have examined in this chapter is not due to a problem in the world: it is God's good design. He desires that it should be this way.

Notably, this is the only section of Ecclesiastes where the word *vanity* (*hebel*) does not appear. Most of the frustrations discussed in the other chapters of the book are due to the senseless absurdities of life (vanity). The problems we encounter in other chapters are problems resulting from the sinfulness of the world. But in this chapter, we have stepped into a different realm of human limitations. The closing phrase of this study—'God desires [of us] what has already been pursued'—is a counterpoint to the familiar conclusion of the book's other studies: 'This also is vanity and a striving after wind' (e.g. 2:26).

God has designed life to have seasons and limits so that we might learn to live in the fear of the Lord. That is his good design, and joyful is the person who learns to live in that faith.

Reading this text, I think about my father and my late grandfather. Both men are models of honest hard work. My grandfather laboured through the Depression and World War II. My father started his career in the post-war decades, entering the computer industry just as the modern computer era was dawning. The fact that my father was better able to provide for his family than my grandfather could provide for his is no reflection on any difference in their skills or commitments or their godliness. Both men feared God, and each worked hard within the circumstances of his time.

But ultimately, it is God who gives us the food, drink and work we enjoy, and it is God who brings all things to his perfect conclusions. What the seasons are like in which we labour is beyond our control. But we are blessed to know the goodness of the God who does control all things. To live in submission to him is truly to live joyfully.

Notes

1 The Hebrew word *zeman* does appear once in this passage. The opening parallelism literally reads, 'For everything there is a *zeman*, and an *'et* for every matter under heaven' (v. 1). It is, nevertheless, the latter term (*'et*) that is repeated twenty-eight more times in the rest of the passage and carries the weight of the poem. Most likely, *zeman* is used in the first line for stylistic reasons, namely because it is the best word available to set up the idea of the poem that its synonym, *'et*, will carry forward. If, however, the writer intends *zeman* to convey its full weight in the first line, one might conclude that the poem affirms God's sovereignty over appointed dates in the first line (something he alone knows), then, in the second line, turns to God's appointment of the general seasons of life, by which human beings discern their proper activities. It is, in either case, the latter idea (the idea expressed by *'et*) which the passage develops.

2 Fox, *A Time to Tear Down*, pp. 198–201.

3 Cf. Paul's metaphorical use of the expression in reference to a late birth in 1 Cor. 15:8.

4 The expression 'eternity in man's heart' is matched with the phrase 'find out what God has done from the beginning to the end'. These two phrases are synonymous, the latter confirming what is meant by the former.

5 Cf. Gordis, *Koheleth*, pp. 146, 223–224.

Reviving hope: vanity and hope in life's dilemmas I (3:16–4:6)

Colour blindness affects 1 out of every 12 men, and 1 out of every 200 women.[1] Among the many tests available for colour blindness, the most common is the Ishihara Color Test. Developed by Japanese researcher Shinobu Ishihara, this test consists of test cards, each of which presents a field of coloured dots. The dots are of various sizes and shades of colour. A person with normal colour acuity will be able to see the shape of a number formed within the field of dots, but a colour-blind person will not be able to discern the number. Examples can be found readily on the Internet.

This next section of Ecclesiastes might be likened to a series of Ishihara Color Test images. There are nine images in Qohelet's series extending from 3:16 to 5:20. But Qohelet is not painting visual images to test our ability to discern colour; he is presenting situational quandaries that exercise our discernment of hope in the midst of life's vanities.

All the world is full of trouble, but there are different shades of vanity in the world. Not all vanities are equally vain. Rather than falling into cynicism (a form of 'hope blindness' analogous to 'colour blindness'), the nine case studies in Ecclesiastes 3:16–5:20 train us to discern the outlines of what is worth affirming in the midst of life's vanities.

The key expression that we will encounter repeatedly in these passages is 'better than that' or other similar phrases. The appearance of the comparison 'better' in each case study is our signal that Qohelet is showing us what is better in the midst of each conundrum. In some cases, it is something better for us to do—that is, it is practical advice. For instance, one scenario presents the practical instruction, 'To draw near to listen [in God's house] is better than to offer the sacrifice of fools' (5:1). Some scenarios resolve with practical instruction on what it is better to do. In other cases, there is no practical guidance given but rather a qualitative valuation we are taught to make. For example, one scenario shows us that 'this is gain for a land in every way: a king committed to cultivated fields' (5:9). This is not practical instruction concerning something to do, but rather the outline of what to hope for and to prize in a ruler.

Qohelet is not a cynic, calling out the absurdity of life without hope. In a process comparable to presenting us with a series of colour test cards, Qohelet's nine case studies provide the outlines of 'what is better' in the midst of otherwise muddled and confusing quandaries. In this chapter, we will take up the first three (3:16–4:6) of Qohelet's nine case studies. The remaining six (three in 4:7–5:7 and three more in 5:8–5:17) will be explored in subsequent chapters, bringing us finally to the call to joy that closes the passage (5:18–20).

The case of corrupt justice (3:16–22)

The first case study Qohelet introduces is the paradox of government corruption, when injustice pervades the halls of justice. One expects to find corruption among criminals, but what is one to do when a society's 'justice' is unjust? This is truly a quandary for those seeking to labour honestly in such lands.

Years ago, I was involved in ministry in a country fraught with corruption. Even Christian ministries were under immense pressure to pay off corrupt officials and provide 'protection money' to mafia groups simply to operate. Maybe in the democratic West, corruption is not so obvious or rampant. But Qohelet's first dilemma raises a real problem experienced in many parts of the world: corrupt governments.

After naming the problem (the 'I saw under the sun' statement in v. 16), Qohelet offers two considerations (the two 'I said in my heart' statements in vv. 17 and 18–21), leading to his conclusion ('So I saw that there is nothing better than …' in v. 22).

The first consideration is deceptively simple: 'I said in my heart, God will judge the righteous and the wicked, for there is a time for every matter and for every work' (v. 17). Human governments may promote wickedness and punish righteousness, but God keeps track of it all and promises to make the final verdict. To state it seems simple; but to believe that it is so is profoundly comforting—and instructive. Though life may become tangled in an impossible web of corruption and injustice, God will one day untangle that web and straighten everything out as it should be. To cling confidently to this certitude is crucial to the conclusion Qohelet will offer when we get to verse 22.

Qohelet's second consideration takes a bit more attention to unpack: 'I said in my heart with regard to the children of man that God is testing them that they may see that they themselves are but beasts. For … as one dies, so dies the other …' (vv. 18–21). Has Qohelet suddenly changed topics on us, switching from the subject of government corruption to the topic of animals and death? No, he is showing us the humbling lesson that we learn from the presence of corruption in human society. It shows how beastly we people can become, left to our sin.

Genesis teaches that mankind was created in the image of God (Gen. 1:26–31). That Genesis passage gives particular emphasis to mankind's reflecting God's likeness as social beings, establishing homes and governing over the creation. Mankind was created to be more than animals, and to establish societies of God-like grace. But when societies fall to animal-like greed and corruption, God uses such occurrences to expose our nature when at our worst, apart from God. The great equalizer—death—grants finality to Qohelet's comparison. Even animals die the same way people do.

There is a two-part comparison that Qohelet makes between people and animals to drive home the sameness of their deaths. First, he compares the sameness of their bodily decay: 'All are from the dust, and to dust all return' (v. 20). Then he compares the sameness of their final breath: 'Who knows whether the spirit [or 'breath'] of man goes upward and the spirit [or 'breath'] of the beast goes down into the earth?' (v. 21). The Hebrew word that can be translated 'spirit' in some contexts is to be translated 'breath' in other contexts. Some interpreters believe Qohelet is speaking of the destination of the human and animal soul in this verse. More likely, though, he is speaking about the expiration (that is, the loss of breath) that marks death.

Some ancient societies believed that human superiority was due to mankind's different breath from that of animals (a view not to be confused with the Genesis account of God's breathing life into mankind). For instance, the ancient Greeks believed that human breath contained a 'spark of the ether' from the gods. At death, human breath would ascend back to the seat of the gods (or into the cosmic ether). An animal's breath, however, was believed to lack this divine spark in its composition and thus, being heavier, would descend into the earth at death.[2] In verse 21, Qohelet calls into question such speculations about a qualitative difference between human breath and that of the animals.

Qohelet is not venturing into lessons on the nature of the human soul.[3] To the contrary, he is pointing out the sameness of human death compared with animal death. He is calling into question speculation that the human breath is something innately superior to that of animals, for the fact is that both die (expire) and decay (return to dust) the exact same way. Qohelet is by no means demeaning the dignity of mankind made in God's image, but he is confronting us with the true beasts we become when our societies turn selfish and corrupt like wild animals.

Actually, the lesson Qohelet here presses upon us to expose our humble condition is the exact same lesson the psalmist ponders to magnify God's grace:

> When I look at your heavens, the work of your fingers,
>> the moon and the stars, which you have set in place,
> what is man that you are mindful of him,
>> and the son of man that you care for him?
> Yet you have made him a little lower than the heavenly beings
>> and crowned him with glory and honour.
> You have given him dominion over the works of your hands;
>> you have put all things under his feet,
> all sheep and oxen,
>> and also the beasts of the field,
> the birds of the heavens, and the fish of the sea,
>> whatever passes along the paths of the seas (Ps. 8:3–8).

To sum up: there are two considerations Qohelet leads us to ponder in the face of corrupt societies. First, we can rest assured that God will reward righteousness and punish evil, even if human governments do not (v. 17). Second, we must learn the lesson corrupt governments force all of us to face: apart from God's grace, we are no different from animals (vv. 18–21).

As with a mathematical equation, Qohelet takes these two considerations, adds them together and produces a powerful result: 'So I saw that there is nothing better than that a man should rejoice in his work, for that is his lot. Who can bring him to see what will be [afterward]?' (v. 22).[4] The powerful insight in this conclusion is the reason given for rejoicing in one's work: 'for that is his lot.'

In English, we use the word 'lot' to refer to a parcel of ground or other kind of property. The Hebrew term (*heleq*; cf. *goral*) also refers to property, especially to the plots of land divided up among the tribes of Israel *by lots* in the days of Joshua (Josh. 13–21). By drawing lots for the land, the people were letting God assign to each tribe its inheritance.

Thus the term 'lot' in Hebrew developed the connotation of any inheritance that God sovereignly assigned to a person.

In other words, God is the one who gives each person his or her place in the world. It is the duty of human governments to serve God by rewarding what God rewards (Rom. 13:1–7). But when governments fail to uphold justice, we still look to God for the final verdict on our labours. Who knows what the outcome of our labours will be? It is God who decides, not human governments. Qohelet's conclusion leaves many questions unanswered. He does not offer promises of social transformation. But that is the elegance of his conclusion: *without* grand promises, he shows us the framework of faith (v. 17) and humility (vv. 18–21) that allows us to apply ourselves to our work with joy (v. 22)—even in a corrupt land.

In the face of the paradox of injustice in the halls of justice, it is better to leave the results to God and faithfully to devote oneself to one's duties.

The case of an oppressive elite (4:1–3)

We have just considered the paradox of corrupt governments. Qohelet's next quandary is related but different. He now speaks of societies where the elite oppress the poor. The resulting paradox is this: in oppressive societies, comfort is given to the oppressors and not to those who are suffering.

Every society has its elite; there is nothing wrong with that. In a well-ordered society, those in positions of influence use their status to comfort the afflicted and care for the needy. Scripture commends those who use their status to minister to the poor (e.g. Isa. 58:6–11; Matt. 25:34–40; 1 Tim. 6:17–19). But the abuse of power is too common to be ignored. And where there is oppression, this paradox emerges: power protects the oppressors and comfort is lacking for their victims.

All forms of social oppression—economic, racial, intellectual, artistic, political or otherwise—are included in 'all the oppressions that are done under the sun' Qohelet has in view. What is worthwhile in the midst of such oppression? Qohelet concludes, 'And I thought the dead who are already dead more fortunate than the living who are still alive. But better than both is he who has not yet been and has not seen the evil deeds that are done under the sun' (vv. 2–3).

Many interpret this answer as hopeless cynicism. One commentator writes, 'Although Qohelet is burdened and grieved by the thought of death, in this same passage despair drives him to prefer it to life … This outburst … comes in a moment of despondency and is not determinative of Qohelet's philosophy.'[5] Is this really an emotional outburst of cynicism in which Qohelet contradicts the love of life evident in the rest of his book? In my view, the fact that Qohelet values life through the rest of the book should raise red flags over an interpretation that understands this text as a fascination with death.

It should be obvious that Qohelet is not telling us what people think before they even exist! He is speaking theoretically about the timeline of human experience, tracing from back to front: 'And I thought [3] *the dead who are already dead* more fortunate than [2] *the living who are still alive*. But better than both is [1] *he who has not yet been* and has not seen the evil deeds that are done under the sun' (emphasis added). It is as though Qohelet is placing a measure at three points along the human timeline, taking a measurement of suffering at each of those points. At the endpoint (after death), the thermometer reading is better than at the midpoint (among those alive under oppression). For the dead, oppression is over, though the memory of that suffering is still there (philosophically speaking, at least; it is doubtful Qohelet imagines that the dead are literally grieving over past oppressions!). The final measurement—the level of suffering among those not yet born—yields the best result of all, since no evil has yet been seen. The whole picture is a caricature and intended to be read as such. How is it possible to speak literally about the suffering of someone who does not yet exist? This is not the emotional outburst of a cynic; it is a vivid reminder that all human oppression has limits—and that looking beyond those limits provides hope for those now alive.

It is those who are alive to whom Qohelet is writing. He is not writing for the benefit of those already dead or those not yet born: he is writing to those alive now. And he comforts us with the assurance that those who have already died are now at rest from their suffering. Oppression can no longer reach them; it is over for them. Best of all, we have hope for future generations that they might never face the suffering we now experience.

Rather than expressing cynicism, Qohelet's 'better than both' conclusion in verse 3 is a word of hope concerning future generations. What is best for those who suffer oppression? To consider with hope and prayer their children and grandchildren. It is that hope which is a source of comfort, even in lands under oppression that has no end in sight.

The case of business greed (4:4–6)

Here is another dilemma. The most effective business ventures are often those done to undermine someone else (v. 4). It is a moral paradox that something as sinister as envy motivates so much accomplishment, while those who lack such motivation accomplish little (v. 5). This problem is captured in modern pop culture by the motto of Gordon Gekko, the lead character in the 1987 film *Wall Street*. 'Greed is good,' was the fictional executive's motto. Qohelet recognizes that there is substance to that statement. Greed is not good, morally; yet it is economically empowering. This is truly a point of enigma (*hebel*) in life.

Let me clarify several points before we look at Qohelet's response to this dilemma. First, we should not absolutize the statement 'all toil and all skill in work come from … envy'. The word translated 'all' here can mean 'every single instance' or 'in all manner of cases'. I take it to be used in the latter sense here. There are exceptions to this general principle. There are those who toil skilfully, motivated by love. Scripture gives us many noble examples, such as Noah with his ark, Solomon with his temple, and the many works of Jesus. Qohelet's 'all' does not indicate an absolute reality but a universal generality. Wherever you go, you will encounter great works of skill motivated by selfishness and pride.

Second, the phrase 'all toil and all skill in work' is not talking about two things. The phrase is a Hebraic way of saying, 'all labour, that is, all skilful work'. The second phrase emphatically restates the first. Qohelet's observation is that envy is what typically motivates invention, improvement and advances in technology. Those who are not envious are content with the status quo. Those who are driven to surpass their neighbours are the ones who develop highly skilled advances.

In Genesis 4 we have a series of examples. The descendants of wicked Cain (not the descendants of peaceful Seth) devised the techniques of nomadic shepherding (Gen. 4:20), invented musical instruments (v. 21) and introduced metallurgy (v. 22). Skill and technological advances should be found among those motivated by love and the glory of God; but, more often than not, it is those striving to advance their own kingdoms who excel. This is not the way it should be, but, sadly, it is often the way it is.

Third, let me clarify the role of the 'fool' in verse 5. This indolent 'fool' serves as a foil to the accomplished entrepreneur in verse 4. It is important to understand that the word 'fool' does not always mean one who is *morally* foolish; the word simply means someone who lacks skill. Someone who lacks the relationship skills or the skills of holiness is indeed a social or moral fool. However, someone who lacks the skills of his trade might be morally upright but a 'fool' in terms of his work. The fool in verse 5 is the person who lacks any yearning to compete with his neighbour and thus never develops the skills to compete. He may be a moral, upright person, but he is unskilled. He folds his hands in indolence and 'eats his own flesh'. Some scholars think that latter phrase means he fretfully chews his knuckles. Others think it refers to his wasting away for lack of food to eat because his envious neighbour is undermining his profits. In either case, his physical deterioration is a vivid reminder that a lack of motivation at work is ultimately self-destructive.

What is the faithful man's solution in the face of this paradox of human labour? Qohelet's answer appears in another 'better than' statement: 'Better is a handful of quietness than two hands full of toil and a striving after wind' (v. 6). With that short line the writer elegantly says just enough to make his point, positioning himself between the envious workaholic on the one side and the indolent simpleton on the other. Notice how Qohelet's solution commends a full hand in opposition to the simpleton's folded hand, but also praises the motivation of quietness in opposition to the super-achiever's envy.

Indolence and lack of skill are disdained. A productive 'handful' is what Qohelet commends. However, despite the super-achievement that is attained through envy, Qohelet still exhorts quietness in labour that achieves a bit less. We are told to work in ways that nurture peace with neighbours, rather than excelling through a culture of strife.

The result is an economic formula that makes no sense mathematically (1 handful > 2 hands full!) but makes great sense when life is lived in the fear of the Lord, trusting that his eternal rewards are not proportional to what is experienced here and now.

The first three quandaries

So far, we have examined three of Qohelet's nine case studies about human labour. I trust it is already becoming obvious that he is doing something extremely important as he wades through such dilemmas with us. Qohelet is teaching us to be realistic about the senselessness (*hebel*) we will encounter in our own lives. We may not face the same dilemmas Qohelet describes, but he is teaching us to discern the 'better way' amid perplexing scenarios in an imperfect world. He is also laying the groundwork for joy vibrant enough to survive—and eclipse—such sorrows.

The Christian faith is not about escaping trouble or securing prosperity. Nor does the Bible give insight to understand all the hard things we experience. We will always face things that don't make sense 'under the sun'. Qohelet is helping us to find joy without glossing over life's many absurdities.

We have not yet reached the crowning conclusion of this lengthy series of paradoxes, where the writer will distil them into another call to joy. But at the close of each individual dilemma, he is already giving us hints of the joy available to those living in the fear of the Lord. Whatever life throws at us, the one who fears God can 'rejoice in his work, [knowing] that is his lot', and trust that 'God will judge [all things] …, for there is a time for every matter and for every work' (3:22, 17).

Notes

1 Statistics from the Colour Blind Awareness organization www.colourblindawareness.org; accessed September 2015.

2 Martin Hengel, *Judaism and Hellenism: Studies in Their Encounter in Palestine During the Early Hellenistic Period* (trans. John Bowden, 2 vols; Minneapolis: Fortress Press, 1974), vol. 1, p. 124. Cf. Fox, *A Time to Tear Down*, p. 215.

3 Later in the book, Qohelet will plainly affirm that mankind does ascend to God's presence at death (12:7).

4 The ESV ends the verse, 'Who can bring him to see what will be after him?' Fox argues persuasively that the translation should be, 'Who can enable him to see what will happen afterward?' The passage is not necessarily pointing ahead to what will happen after a person's death, but to uncertainty about what will happen after any given task. Fox, *A Time to Tear Down*, pp. 214, 217.

5 Fox, *A Time to Tear Down*, p. 220.

Restoring value: vanity and hope in life's dilemmas II (4:7–5:7)

Many great thinkers of the ancient world used paradoxes to teach. Aristotle (c.384–322 BC) famously developed the 'Wheel Paradox', an imagined scenario of rolling two wheels of different sizes the same distance, in order to teach a lesson on geometry. Zeno (c.490–430 BC) posed the 'Arrow Paradox' and the parable of 'Achilles and the Tortoise' to teach his students about the nature of motion. Telling a pithy story with a paradoxical twist is a useful way to engage a student's understanding.

The paradoxes of Aristotle and Zeno are exercises for teaching principles of mathematics and physics. Qohelet has prepared a series of case studies that teach us about labouring in hope. Qohelet's paradoxes train us to think about challenges we face as we work in an imperfect world, and to discern the path of godliness and joy.

In the last chapter, we explored the first three of these case studies. We now examine three more.

The case of the rich loner (4:7–12)

In this example, we meet a hard-working loner. He is a self-made man with no collaborators and no dependents—neither son nor brother. His income is his alone. But here is the dilemma: even though he does not have to divide his profits with others, he is the poorer for working alone. We could put Qohelet's finding in the following mathematical formula:

($x ÷ 1 person) < ($x ÷ 2 people). That makes no sense mathematically, but Qohelet shows that it is true.

First of all, he tells us why independent labour is less rewarding than teamwork.[1] There are two reasons why a person works when alone. He or she might labour to *accomplish* something. But there is always more that needs to be done: 'there is no end to all his toil' (v. 8). So, if this person seeks fulfilment through accomplishment, he or she will never attain it. A person also labours for *income*. But there is always more to earn: 'his eyes are never satisfied with riches' (v. 8). Neither accomplishment nor wealth are goals that can be completed. Both, Qohelet shows us, are goals with infinite dimensions. Independent labour seeks joy in accomplishment or wealth, rather than asking, '*For whom* am I toiling and depriving myself of pleasure?' Such labour is, in the words of Qohelet, 'vanity [*hebel*] and an unhappy business' (v. 8).

What gives labour its fullest sense of reward is when achievement and income are accomplished in camaraderie—working with and for others. 'Two are better than one, because they have a good reward for their toil' (v. 9). Qohelet does not suggest that two produce more profits than one. The examples he gives of their 'good reward' are not monetary but relational: 'For if they fall, one will lift up his fellow'; 'they keep warm [together]'; and in the face of an enemy, 'two will withstand him—a threefold cord is not quickly broken' (vv. 10–12). These are not promises of greater income or greater accomplishment; they are the rewards of fellowship.

Certainly, there are exceptions to this principle. There are loners who are happy working by themselves and for themselves. But as a general principle, Qohelet's point reminds us that God made us for work and for relationships (Gen. 1:26–30). We fulfil our God-given design only as we develop both together.

It is through labour that wealth is created. Limiting wealth's division seems advantageous. Nevertheless, paradoxical as it may seem, Qohelet advises that labour shared is more rewarding than wealth that is not shared.

The case of the forgotten sage (4:13–16)

Qohelet uses a story to introduce his next lesson. Some believe that Solomon is talking about his father, David, who replaced foolish King Saul. Others think this story is about someone unknown to us. After all, the passage says, 'those who come later will not rejoice in him' (v. 16). In other words, the wise youth of this story is forgotten to history.

But there is another possibility. There is a youth spoken of in Scripture who rose to power, and whose name is remembered among the people of God but forgotten among the people he served. Maybe Qohelet is referring to Joseph. Notice the parallels between Qohelet's story and the Genesis account of Joseph's life.

Joseph 'went from prison to the throne [in Egypt], though in his own kingdom he had been poor' (v. 14). Joseph was never king of Egypt, but he sat on the throne as Egypt's second-in-command. He became the prime minister (or vizier) of the land.

Genesis tells us that Pharaoh sent two of his officers into prison while Joseph was there (Gen. 40:1–4). Perhaps Qohelet has that action in mind when he says that the old king 'no longer knew how to take advice' (v. 13). It is a proud king who imprisons courtiers when they voice criticism.

When Joseph did become prime minister, 'There was no end of all the people, all of whom he led' (v. 16). Egypt was one of the greatest nations on earth, and its population was vast. Joseph ruled wisely, delivering the people from the impact of a great famine. Yet in spite of all the good he did, Joseph's name was forgotten. In ancient lands, rulers who fell out of favour with succeeding generations were deliberately forgotten. Their monuments were erased, their names forbidden and their place in history eradicated by fiat. That might be what the book of Exodus means when it records, 'there arose a new king over Egypt, who did not know Joseph'

(Exod. 1:8). As a foreigner ruling Egypt, Joseph would have been an embarrassment of Egyptian history. Most likely, his name was forgotten deliberately.

Whomever Qohelet has in mind, if it is not Joseph, it is someone whose experience was similar to that of Joseph. Qohelet uses this story to illustrate another paradox of life in this broken world: too often, people honour the fool who has the trappings of glory, and they forget the wise.

That is one of life's tragedies. It is not the way it should be; it is 'vanity and a striving after wind' (v. 16). Praise God, there are exceptions to this injustice. But the problem was not only in Joseph's day and Qohelet's time, but persists in our own. Even so, Qohelet exhorts us to take his counsel on what is better. Wisdom is better than prestige.

The case of the pious fool (5:1–7)

In these paragraphs, we have one of the most sobering dilemmas so far. To make sense of this passage, we first need to understand the role of *vows* in Old Testament worship.

A good example is the story of Jacob's vow at Bethel (Gen. 28:10–22). Jacob had left his father's house, literally running for his life. His older brother, Esau, wanted to kill him. So Jacob fled to seek refuge with distant relatives. During the first night of Jacob's dangerous and uncertain exile, the Lord spoke to him in a dream.

Jacob had a vision of angels ascending and descending a ladder over him, with the Lord himself at the top of the ladder. Even though Jacob thought he was alone on this journey, in reality God was watching over him. Jacob realized he was not alone after all.

In response to this promise of God's blessing on his venture,

> Jacob made a vow, saying, 'If God will be with me and will keep me in this way that I go, and will give me bread to eat and clothing to wear, so that I come again to my father's house in peace, then the LORD shall be my God, and this

stone, which I have set up for a pillar, shall be God's house. And of all that you give me I will give a full tenth to you' (Gen. 28:20–22).

Was Jacob negotiating with God? Was he bribing God to look after him? No. God had already given Jacob a promise of his constant attention and care. Jacob was not making a vow to buy God's protection. Because God had already promised to bless his journey, Jacob vowed that if—or, as the word could also be translated, when—he returned in safety, he would bring God a tenth of all his profit in recognition that God's blessing had made him to prosper. That is the nature of a vow in Old Testament worship.

In the face of some great venture—including business ventures—a pious Hebrew would seek God's blessing on his work. If the task was dangerous or risky, the motivation to seek God's favour was greater. A vow was a promise to God of a percentage (as with Jacob) or of some other fruit from the project. It was a statement at the beginning that the person would thank God at the other end according to God's blessing on the work. Carried out properly, this was simply an expression of devotion with a promise of thanks. It was a holy and honourable aspect of worship. But sometimes, less spiritual businessmen looked at vows as a way to bribe God—to negotiate his blessing by promising him something if he did bless.

It is against this backdrop that Qohelet introduces his next quandary of human labour. Some of those who seek God's blessing on their work actually increase his wrath against them by doing so. It would be better for them to pursue their ventures without praying for God's blessing, than to seek his blessing with such an attitude.

Every time we come to God's house, we should 'draw near to listen' (v. 1). Rather than hastily pouring out our requests, we should take time to hear his words to us. Qohelet is not discouraging prayer; he is reminding us to approach God as servants before a mighty king: 'God is in heaven and you are on earth' (v. 2). He commands us and he makes gracious promises to us. Our prayers are to be in response to his promises and in service of his commands.

Twice in the passage, Qohelet likens a fool's words to God (that is, his prayers) to dreams (vv. 3, 7). A dream is full of activity and feelings, but when you wake up it all evaporates. So it is with a fool's words to God. They are many and full of emotion, but they are empty. Such vain worshippers 'do not know that they are doing evil' (v. 1). Rather than being pleased with their prayers and blessing their labours, 'God [is] angry at [their] voice and destroy[s] the work of [their] hands' (v. 6). Those are strong words leading us to Qohelet's paradox: empty prayers for God's blessing actually bring the opposite (cf. Isa. 1:11–18). It is better to make no vows to God than to speak many words we will later abandon (v. 5).

Qohelet does not seek to scare us from worship. Rather, he calls us to worship in true devotion. And when God does bless our labours, we ought to be genuine and faithful in thanking him.

Three quandaries

A friend of mine used to flip houses for a living. He would buy a house inexpensively, fix it up and resell it for more. The secret, he told me, could be summed up in three words. First, put up *trim* to make the walls look good. Then, use *caulk* to hide cracks the trim does not hide. Finally, *paint* to cover everything else. It is typical of us human beings to focus on what looks good: lots of money, prestige and glory—and a show of piety.

In the three snapshots of human labour covered in this study, Qohelet is training us to look deeper. He is showing us that there are cracks in the way the world works that cannot simply be caulked and painted over. Our calling is to pursue the 'better' way through the resulting dilemmas: to labour in communion, to pursue wisdom over prestige, and to reverently worship God rather than expecting God to serve us.

These are profound lessons that pave the road to a life of godly joy.

Notes

1 Sometimes portions of this text are quoted in wedding ceremonies. The theme of sharing evoked by this passage fits nicely with marriage, but this is a passage about vocation, not marriage. It is about collaboration in the workshop, camping out in the sheep fields, and toiling side-by-side in other career pursuits. This is especially clear when we come to the punchline of the passage. After repeatedly describing the strengths of two working together, in the last line Qohelet ups the number to three. He clearly does not have marriage in mind in this passage, but vocational collaboration.

Renewing joy: vanity and hope in life's dilemmas III (5:8–20)

On 22 November 1928 the Paris Opéra performed the premiere of Maurice Ravel's orchestral masterpiece, *Boléro*. It was a stunning success—even though the music simply repeats the same melodic line over and over for close to fifteen minutes.

When the idea for *Boléro* first occurred to Ravel, he played the melody line to a friend and said, 'I'm going to try and repeat it a number of times without any development, gradually increasing the orchestra as best I can.'[1] And that is exactly what he did. The music begins with a flute playing the theme. As the flute repeats the theme over and over, other instruments gradually join in. The theme never changes, but the whole performance builds and intensifies—for fifteen minutes.

Qohelet's nine case studies of labour follow a similar pattern. The theme of these quandaries never changes: all labour under the sun is vanity and striving after wind, *yet there is hope worth pursuing*. Each case study presents a real dilemma, but by showing us the 'better way' through each dilemma, Qohelet teaches us to conduct our own work in the fear of the Lord.

In this chapter, as we come to the last three case studies, Qohelet increases the intensity. Like Ravel's *Boléro*, Qohelet's paradoxes continue the same lesson but intensify as we come to the climax. This increased intensity is evidenced in his changed terminology. Previously, Qohelet used the phrase 'better than' to introduce his solution to each dilemma. In the last three dilemmas, however, that phrase is replaced by more dramatic variations: 'this is gain for a land' (v. 9); 'what advantage [is it] …?' (v. 11); and 'what gain is there …?' (v. 16).

Like Ravel's addition of woodwind instruments and trumpets towards the end of *Boléro*, Qohelet raises the intensity of our struggle with work's confusing dilemmas as we near the end. But unlike *Boléro*, which simply stops, Qohelet's masterpiece breaks into a glorious chorus of joy at its climax. We can look forward to that call to joy as we complete the last three case studies.

The case of bloated bureaucracies (5:8–9)

Management is a good thing. God designed human beings to organize themselves into teams, with some filling oversight roles and others working in support roles. The seeds of human hierarchies are already present in the order established at creation (Gen. 2:4–24).[2] Such collaboration is the very nature of the triune God, who accomplishes his work in three persons (Father, Son and Holy Spirit) leading and serving one another.[3] He made us, human beings, to be productive as we labour in teams and societies. But in this broken world, hierarchies often become bloated and undermine fruitfulness. That is the paradox Qohelet confronts next. The very structures of society designed to enhance the fruitfulness of labour often do the opposite.

In these verses, Qohelet talks about kings and government bureaucracies, but his lesson applies to business hierarchies too. In the ancient world, government and business were not separated as distinctly as in the West today. The king's job included the oversight and development of businesses. Qohelet points to this concern in his commendation of kings 'committed to cultivated fields' (v. 9). This case study is framed in terms of political bureaucracies, but it is applicable to businesses too.

Qohelet (himself a king) acknowledges this dilemma: the very bureaucracies designed to promote the land's productivity sometimes become a great drain on the land. This situation is not good. But when it happens, Qohelet advises us not to fret about it: 'do not be amazed at the matter' (v. 8). Such bureaucratic breakdowns are to be expected in this vain (*hebel*) world, and you might not be able to do anything about it.

Qohelet warns, 'the high official is watched by a higher, and there are yet higher ones over them' (v. 8). This observation is not describing positive checks and balances. Praise God when a bureaucracy does have built-in accountability that is working! But that is not the case in Qohelet's picture. What our text describes is a bloated bureaucracy committed to its own preservation rather than to the productivity of the land. The self-interest of low officials is often *protected* by higher officials. The 'watching over' traced out in this passage describes one level of bureaucracy protecting the underlings who work for them.

Notice how Qohelet begins with the abuse of power one sees 'in a province' (that is, locally). If you appeal to a higher official, you may discover that the higher official is watching out for the lower one. All through the system, bureaucrats seek their own ends and, through a network of obligations to one another, cover for each other. Instead of holding each other accountable for the benefit of the whole organization's productivity, bureaucracies have a tendency to become self-preserving.

How much better it is ('gain for a land in every way') when there is a king who is 'committed to cultivated fields' (v. 9). In one beautiful expression, Qohelet topples the whole system of corruption with his vision of a king whose care is, quite literally, for success at the 'grass roots'.

Franz Delitzsch explains, 'An agriculture-king [is] one who is addicted, not to wars, lawsuits, and sovereign stubbornness in his opinions, but who delights in the peaceful advancement of the prosperity of his country ...'[4] Such kings—and corporate CEOs—are hard to find. Even when a ruler begins well, pride often follows. King Uzziah is a classic example: 'And he built towers in the wilderness and cut out many cisterns, for he had large herds, both in the Shephelah and in the plain, and he had farmers and vinedressers in the hills and in the fertile lands, *for he loved the soil* … But when he was strong, he grew proud, to his destruction' (2 Chr. 26:10, 16, emphasis added).

We ought not to be shocked ('do not be amazed', v. 8) when the very structures designed to increase productivity end up becoming a great drain instead. But neither should we fall into cynicism against all bureaucracy. Qohelet calls us to cling to the doctrine that management is good, and that a land (or company) is greatly blessed to have management. But he holds out to us the prayer and hope for management committed to the land, not to bureaucratic self-preservation.

Qohelet's 'better way' under a bloated bureaucracy is to be patient in an imperfect situation, to guard against cynicism, and to hope and pray for 'a king committed to cultivated fields' (v. 9).

The case of growing appetites (5:10–12)

With a note of humour, Qohelet's next description caricatures the absurdity of wealth. People seek wealth to satisfy their appetites, but once wealth is attained, it actually increases that appetite. Seeking wealth is like eating potato chips: you start because they look so satisfying, but the more you have, the more you want. This is the paradox of humanity's appetite for wealth.

By God's grace, there are wealthy individuals who learn contentment. Statements like this are not designed to present an invariable law. Such descriptions do, however, capture a real absurdity of life under the sun. Wealth tends to whet the appetite rather than satisfy it.

That is not all. Qohelet seems to be grinning as he adds another layer to the example: 'When goods increase, they increase who eat them, and what advantage has their owner but to see them with his eyes?' (v. 11). When someone wins the lottery, long-lost relatives suddenly turn up needing money. The risk of theft also increases as wealth increases.

Overhead costs go up. In Solomon's day, wealth kept in gold had to be guarded (at a cost), and wealth maintained in flocks and cattle had to be tended (at a cost). Even today, money kept in various investments has to be managed, with an increased number of hired accountants required. With a tone of irony, Qohelet declares that so many other people end up managing, controlling and eating off the rich man's wealth that the owner's 'only' privilege is to look on and see the goods from which others benefit (v. 11). He is speaking in hyperbole; but his point introduces a further dimension to the paradox of appetite. Increasing wealth only increases the rich man's own appetite; meanwhile, his wealth serves to satisfy the appetites of others who eat off his increase!

Of course, Qohelet is being ironic. There is much that an owner does gain from his wealth (recall the pleasures of Eccles. 2). Nevertheless, in this comical picture of the wrong appetites sated through the rich man's wealth, Qohelet captures one of the true vanities of labour. And he sets the stage to teach us a better way: 'Sweet is the sleep of a labourer, whether he eats little or much, but the full stomach of the rich will not let him sleep' (v. 12).

Here is a radical change in focus. Rather than focusing on labour's reward for our stomach, the proper reward to seek is a good night's sleep. Happy is the man who labours to be satisfied in his work (not in work's rewards). Satisfaction of a job well done is the reward every labourer can enjoy, 'whether he eats little or much'; and it is this reward that the greedy lose because of their full stomachs.

There is nothing wrong with a full stomach (or with wealth). The labouring man's sleep is sweet, 'whether he eats little or much'. But Qohelet draws our hearts to labour under different motivations than those of the one whose appetite is for profit. The better way is to seek the satisfaction of faithful labour punctuated by godly rest.

The case of wealth gained and lost (5:13–17)

We come to Qohelet's final case study: the dilemma of loss. He captures this lesson in the tale of a man who slowly built up his estate over a lifetime of toil. The expression 'riches were kept by their owner *to his hurt*' (emphasis added) means that he never enjoyed his earnings himself. He laboured sacrificially and saved frugally to his own detriment. Then, in one bad venture, he lost everything. As a result, he has no inheritance to leave to his son, and he will die penniless. Do you see the layers of tragedy in this narrative? Here is a man who experienced all the toil of building an estate, yet who has nothing to show for it.

'Moreover,' Qohelet introduces a final twist of this tragedy, 'all his [remaining] days he eats in darkness in much vexation and sickness and anger' (v. 17). This is the paradox: a poor man *who never possessed wealth* might have a peaceful end, but the poor man *who was once rich* ends his life in bitterness and grief. His impoverished end is worse for his having gained so much before.

There is no sin here. This is not a cruel miser. In fact, this man's story is a noble portrait: he is a hard worker who restrains his appetites to save for his children's benefit. This final paradox is truly a tragedy and a picture of labour's unpredictable inanity under the sun. The chance failure of one venture wiped everything out. It could have happened to anyone. It most certainly should not have happened to this one. But that is the nature of loss, and many experience its bite.

This final quandary ends differently from the previous eight. There is no 'better way' offered at the close of this case study. We are simply left with the haunting question, 'What gain is there to him who toils for the wind?' (v. 16). The intensity of Qohelet's nine paradoxes reaches a high point of absurdity with this final admission that labour has no reliable value in a world where loss strikes with such cruelty and senselessness.

The unanswered question of the ninth dilemma opens our hearts to hear the only sure way to joy in the midst of all our paradoxes with work in this vain world. The chorus of joy that follows next is both an exalted response to the paradox of loss and a capstone to the whole series of dilemmas leading to this point.

Call to joy (5:18–20)

Qohelet caps off this section with a two-part call to joy. First (in v. 18), he calls us to foster the joy of working as God's servants. There is joy in our toil *when we know that our work is allotted to us by God*. The days he has called us to serve him in this world are limited ('the few days of his life that God has given him'), so we can face life's absurdities with patience.

This is not an answer that fixes the vanity of life under the sun. It is, however, an answer that lifts our eyes above present uncertainties to anchor our hearts in God's goodness. It is, in short, a call to faith. A Christian whose faith in God's sovereignty permeates his or her daily labours can weather the vanities of this-worldly labour with joy.

Think of the man who works hard at his job, receiving no thanks and little pay. But he goes home every night to a wife and child who love and appreciate him. The toil takes on worth, despite its heartaches, because of those for whom he is working. Qohelet is teaching us to labour with the love of God as the source of our joy. It is at home with God, in his presence, that we expect our eternal reward. Even in the most painful and lonely circumstances in this vain world 'under the sun', knowing that God has sovereignly appointed each to his or her lot in life gives us the basis for real joy.

In the second part of this passage (v. 19), we are reminded that life often does bring rewards. We can rest in the Lord when there are no this-worldly rewards; but thankfully, life often is filled with happy benefits and our labour often is rewarded with pleasant returns. For those who do prosper through their labour, Qohelet calls them to acknowledge that 'this is the gift of God'.

Our prosperity doesn't result because we figured out the right techniques to make our work prosper in comparison with others who have not prospered. Many laboured just as diligently as we did—many have laboured more honourably that we did—yet without profiting. Proper work disciplines like diligence and skill *should* bring results, but in this vain world, when those results do come, we should thank God. They are a gift from him, not a mark of our skill.

Verse 20 closes the passage by extolling the practical value of joy for all who find it. Whatever our lot in life—whether wealth or poverty—joy in the heart is given by God to salve the many vanities of our days. It is a great kindness that Qohelet ministers to us through this book, teaching us the way of joy to ease our burdens in this world of vanity.

Notes

1 Arbie Orenstein, *Ravel: Man and Musician* (Mineola, NY: Dover, 1991), p. 98.

2 The leadership of Adam over his wife is about much more than male headship. Adam's leadership over the woman as his close help, and over the animals as well, is a creational paradigm for human society developing under a king (represented by Adam) with families (represented by the woman, as the bearer of children) serving under the ruler, and the rest of the creation (as represented by the animals) serving under humankind in tilling ground and providing raw materials for food and clothing. The hierarchies in Genesis 2 are a microcosm of social order—with collaboration and management—further developed in the rest of biblical history.

3 Philip Ryken and Michael LeFebvre, *Our Triune God: Living in the Love of the Three-in-One* (Wheaton, IL: Crossway, 2011), p. 92.

4 F. Delitzsch, *Commentary on The Song of Songs and Ecclesiastes* (trans. M. G. Easton; Grand Rapids: Eerdmans, 1978 reprint), p. 295.

Working with joy: contentment and the vanities of labour (6:1–9)

When keeping house for a family, it seems there is always laundry to be done. There are always dishes to be washed. There are always rooms to be tidied and straightened. Then, once the laundry is finished, the dishes are done and the toys are stowed away, the cycle starts all over again. Even the most basic chores of life are marked by vanity and striving after wind.

What is worth the investment of one's devotion and energy in a world where nothing is permanent, nothing is certain, and all the fruits of our labours eventually deteriorate? Ultimately, our joy must be grounded in something that is permanent, certain and abiding. Our fleeting labours take on meaning only when we pursue them in the fear of the Lord, serving his purposes and trusting his promises. The Lord is the one who makes 'everything beautiful in its time' (3:11).

As we come to the end of the first half of Ecclesiastes, we come to the end of Qohelet's lessons on joy in our work. In the prologue (1:1–18), two major topics of study were introduced: the vanity of human labour, and the vanity of human wisdom. We now complete the first of those topics. Ecclesiastes 6:1–9 is a conclusion to the studies of human labour in Ecclesiastes 2:1–5:20. In these verses, Qohelet sums things up with a parable.

The vanity of labour without joy (6:1–6)

A single contrast serves to sum up our findings on human labour. It is a bizarre contrast. Qohelet is deliberately exaggerating to make his final point on this topic.

On the one hand, he describes a man who possesses everything the heart could desire: wealth, property and prestige. But for some undisclosed reason, it is someone else who enjoys it all. It does not matter whether ill-health, legal complications or some other reason led to the rich man's inability to enjoy his wealth. Qohelet does not give us a reason for this tragedy; he is painting in abstract strokes. We have a man who possesses everything but enjoys nothing. It is absurd and tragic (v. 2), and the parable gets more bizarre.

In verse 3, Qohelet adds more exaggeration to the picture. He asks us to imagine that this man has a hundred children and lives many years— even 'a thousand years twice over' (v. 6). Obviously this is hyperbole; Qohelet is stretching our imagination. Maybe to modern readers, the thought of a hundred children is more off-putting than enamouring, but in ancient Israel a man's family was a sign—indeed, a means—of his wealth. Children were the family workforce; many children meant more fields tilled and increased production.

Qohelet is painting an unrealistic portrait of ideal wealth and long life to accumulate it. Yet it is ideal wealth with no ability to enjoy it. The crowning mark of this tragic life is the dishonour of his death: 'he also has no burial' (v. 3). To have no burial means no one mourns his loss. Not only did he have no joy in his own life, but also he brought no joy to anyone else. This imaginary caricature is an intentionally exaggerated picture of absolute wealth with the utter absence of satisfaction.

Qohelet sets this imaginary person on one side, and then contrasts him with 'the stillborn child … [who] comes in vanity and goes in darkness, and in darkness its name is covered' (v. 4). We are supposed to imagine the two individuals born at the same time: one of them passing immediately to his eternal rest, and the other going on to a long and prosperous—but unsatisfying—life before dying. Both end up in the same place (death). Which has taken the better route to get there?

Qohelet's scenario is completely hypothetical, and not to be overpressed as a basis for developing conclusions about stillborn children or wealthy tycoons. It is a parable that raises a striking point: the person who bypasses the sorrows of life and enters the eternal rest right away is better off than the wealthiest man who ever lived, if he had no joy in that prosperous life (v. 5). The point of this bizarre contrast is not to exalt death over life; it is to exalt joy over wealth.

We are misguided if we think that God gave us work to do in order that we might enrich ourselves. Wealth, property and honour are not the chief end of work. Nor is pleasure the chief end of work. We must not confuse Qohelet's commendations of joy with the pursuit of pleasure. Ecclesiastes 2 was all about the vanity of working for pleasure. Surely the rich man in Qohelet's parable had many pleasures, but he had no satisfaction—no deep, abiding joy—from all his works.

Qohelet commends us to pursue joy in our work, but not to fall into the traps that ensnare us in vain expectations.

The joy of contentment (6:7–9)

These verses bring Qohelet's final parable on human labour to application. There is nothing new stated here; Qohelet sums up points from our study of labour.

Human appetite (that is, the lust for gain) is never satisfied (v. 7). On this score, the wise man (that is, the person who knows how to make wealth) is no better off than the incompetent fool who cannot earn a dime (v. 8). Wise skills certainly are an advantage over incompetence, but if both are driven by appetite, neither will be satisfied. So what good is it to be more skilful than another, if appetite is the reason for human labour?

The poor man who knows how to make his way in the world might have reason to anticipate an improvement in his economic standing (v. 8). But will that improvement in his standing translate into peace and satisfaction? Not in this vain world—at least, not if appetite is the driving measurement of joy in a person's life.

In his final 'better than' statement in these passages on work, Qohelet closes this study on labour with a simple exhortation to contentment: 'Better is the sight of the eyes than the wandering of the appetite', since following one's appetite is 'vanity and a striving after wind' (v. 9).

There *is* great joy to be found in our work in this world. And it *is* better to labour with skill than with incompetent folly. But the fear of the Lord—pursuing joy by labouring in light of his promises—will transform our natural appetite into contentment. The fruit of following godly principles of labour is not increased profit, but joyful contentment.

Maybe the Apostle Paul had this passage of Ecclesiastes in mind when he wrote similar counsel to young Timothy. In his first epistle to the New Testament pastor, Paul wrote,

> But godliness with contentment is great gain, for we brought nothing into the world, and we cannot take anything out of the world. But if we have food and clothing, with these we will be content. But those who desire to be rich fall into temptation, into a snare, into many senseless and harmful desires that plunge people into ruin and destruction. For the love of money is a root of all kinds of evils. It is through this craving that some have wandered away from the faith and pierced themselves with many pangs (1 Tim. 6:6–10).

You and I live in a world absorbed in the pursuit of wealth. Qohelet calls us to something else: to live in the fear of the Lord, resting in his goodness for our joy. The satisfying fruit of such faith is contentment.

Labour's vanity today

Ecclesiastes' questions about the vanities of labour are timeless. They are the same questions that continue to face philosophers, factory workers, business executives, students, homemakers, and everyone who experiences the weariness of labour today. Some are more conscious of the questions; others feel the weight of these questions without the ability to articulate them. But anyone who recognizes that work is not just physically tiring but also emotionally wearisome is wrestling with the vanity of human toil.

One influential thinker who wrestled with these questions in recent generations was the French philosopher Albert Camus (1913–1960). Camus developed a philosophical system called absurdism, and his ideas greatly influenced the rise of contemporary postmodernism.

Camus's defining work on absurdism was his 1942 book *The Myth of Sisyphus*. He named the book after a character from Greek mythology. According to Greek myth, Sisyphus was condemned by the gods to an endless life of rolling a stone up a mountain, only to see it roll back down and have to repeat the task forever. Camus believed that the myth of Sisyphus captured the absurdity of all human labour as fleeting and meaningless. In many ways, Camus's observations were the same as those of Qohelet; but his conclusions were radically different from Qohelet's.

The reason life in the world is absurd, according to Camus, is because human beings are rational and long for meaning, while the world, in reality, lacks any meaning. Therefore, Camus envisioned only three possibilities. His first possibility is shocking, and thankfully Camus did not recommend it; but the first way a human being can end the absurdity of life, according to Camus, is to end life. Thankfully, Camus did not endorse suicide—he was rightly horrified at the idea. But he expressed this as one way a human can stop the absurdity of 'pushing rocks up mountains'.

The second option Camus acknowledged is the one Qohelet commends: to embrace the hope of God's sovereign purposes. Camus recognized that religious faith provides a solution to the absurdity of life. Just as a child finds comfort in trusting the wisdom of a parent even when that child is unable to understand all that the parent has in mind, so 'the fear of the Lord' offers a real solution to the problem of life's absurdity. But Camus was unwilling to trust that Someone Else—that is, God—has good and beautiful reasons that transcend life's experienced frailties. He rejected the traditional role of faith as the basis for meaning in an absurd world.

Instead, Camus introduced a third option which has captured the imagination of our age. According to Camus, the way to become 'a happy Sisyphus' is to admit that our labours are all absurd, to reject any hope of eternal justice, and to live for the moment with passion. 'What counts,' Camus argued, 'is not the best living but the most living.'[1]

With Camus and others like him, there emerged the contemporary emphases on 'living for the moment', 'creating your own meaning in life', 'following your passions' and living in 'authenticity' to yourself *rather than* submitting to the divine instruction of who we ought to become. Highfalutin terms like existentialism, nihilism and postmodernism all draw upon the same basic ideas about life's vanity expressed by Camus in his philosophy of absurdism.

Three thousand years before Albert Camus, Qohelet had already identified the absurdity of human labour. But he offers us a very different solution from the ephemeral pursuits that characterize our postmodern age. Standing on the long history of Israel's experience of the faithfulness of God, Qohelet calls us to trust God.

Abraham wandered the Promised Land, spending his whole life surveying a land he would never own. But his life was not in vain, because God was laying foundations in Abraham's faithful labours that bore fruit in later generations. Moses abandoned the wealth of Egypt to share in the poverty of an enslaved people, only to wander with them into the wilderness, where his life ended. But, by faith, he understood that God was doing something beautiful through his fleeting labours. Hebrews 11:1–12:2 catalogues thirty-eight examples of saints, from the beginning of the world to the sufferings of Christ himself on the cross, as models of persevering in faith. Once we realize that the Bible is not a single book but a vast collection of testimonies of God's faithfulness across the ages, we gain the perspective for living our own lives in the same faith as Abraham, Moses and others.

I encourage you to consider the faithfulness of God. Study his works of faithfulness throughout the Scriptures in daily devotions and in weekly worship. Continually refresh your heart in his eternal purposes and his abiding love. It is through a reverent fear of the Lord that you will guard your heart from the cynicism and selfishness of a culture awash in postmodern 'solutions' to life's absurdity. Albert Camus and others like him have rightly diagnosed the problem of labour's absurdity, but they fail to appreciate the joy of faith in God who has proven his trustworthiness. It is this solution to the vanity of labour that is commended to us by the ancient philosopher Qohelet.

At the midpoint

We have reached the exact midpoint of Ecclesiastes. There are 222 verses in Ecclesiastes: 111 verses from Ecclesiastes 1:1–6:9, and another 111 from Ecclesiastes 6:10–12:14.[2] We are now literally at the halfway point in Ecclesiastes. It is also the point at which the book changes subject.

Bible scholar Addison Wright explains, 'The book is divided into two main parts … and the thought is also thus divided: in the first part Qohelet is concerned with the vanity of various human endeavors, and in the second part with man's inability to understand the work of God.'[3] In other words, we move from the vanity of human labour to the vanity of human wisdom.

With this change of topic, we leave behind the frequent references to 'work', 'toil' and the concern with 'striving after wind' encountered in the first half of the book. Ecclesiastes 6:9 is the last time the phrase 'striving after wind' appears in the book. We have completed our examination of the question, 'What is good for man *to do*?' (introduced in 2:3).

Now a new set of questions is introduced: 'For who knows what is good for man …? For who can tell man what will be after him under the sun?' (6:12). The catchphrases we will now begin to encounter are expressions like 'to search', 'to find out' and 'to know'. Our attention turns from the work of our hands and the appetite to produce, to the work of our minds and the desire to understand.

Of course, the realms of physical labour and of intellectual thought are not completely isolated from one another. Wisdom and folly were concerns in the earlier half of the book (e.g. 2:12–13), and labour will be discussed in the latter half of the book (e.g. 9:9–10). But the shift of emphasis is unmistakable. We now embark on the second half of Qohelet's quest: the yearning to understand.

Notes

1 Albert Camus, *The Myth of Sisyphus and Other Essays* (New York: Alfred A. Knopf, 1983), p. 61.

2 The verse counts are based on the Hebrew versification of the text. Cf. Wright, 'The Riddle of the Sphinx Revisited', p. 43.

3 Wright, 'The Riddle of the Sphinx: The Structure', p. 324; cf. Wright, 'The Riddle of the Sphinx Revisited', pp. 38–39.

Part 2
Lessons on wisdom

In pursuit of understanding: the vanity and value of wisdom I (6:10–7:18)

The book of Genesis recounts a severe famine in the days of Joseph. The famine impacted the whole Mediterranean world (Gen. 41:57). We can only imagine the untold stories of sorrow and devastation, as well as charity and hope that took place among the myriads of households touched by that seven-year drought.

One question every family would have faced in that famine was the obvious one: What do we do? In a time of famine, what do we do to feed ourselves? Such 'what to do' questions are critical. But another question must have lurked behind that one: *Why* are we suffering this terrible disaster? There must have been a reason for the famine. There would have been natural reasons: certain forces of nature led to a decrease in rainfall, bringing on the famine. There were also supernatural reasons: God was at work, using that famine to accomplish his purposes.[1] In addition to the 'what to do' questions there must have been 'why' questions.

Genesis tells us only one of God's purposes for that particular famine. God was at work in the famine reconciling Joseph's broken family (Gen. 42–47). Joseph's story shows us enough to trust that God's wisdom was at work in every detail of that worldwide famine, even though the Bible tells us nothing about God's specific purposes for each of the thousands upon thousands of other families suffering through that same disaster. In what we are told, we learn enough to know that we can trust God without understanding the rest. But there are many 'why' questions that we cannot answer.

It is when we step behind the 'what to do' issues of life and begin to face such 'why' questions that we enter the realm of wisdom. Wisdom seeks to understand how the world works. Such wisdom, however, is never far from the 'what to do' questions of life. When a farmer better understands why the rain falls when it does and how the soil grows its crops (the questions of wisdom), he will have better answers for the 'what to do' questions about tending his farm through changing seasons. We must not think of biblical wisdom as a heady pursuit. Wisdom is a practical endeavour, but one rooted in the quest to understand.

But is it possible to understand this vain and confusing world? As we enter the second half of Ecclesiastes, Qohelet takes off his workman's hard hat and puts on his philosopher's thinking cap, leaving behind 'what to do' questions to help us face life's 'why' questions.

Wisdom's limit (6:10–12)

Qohelet opens his school of wisdom with a caution about wisdom's limits (vv. 10–12). Qohelet's words in this paragraph can be likened to a puzzle with three pieces. The shape and colour of the first piece is known to us: it is *the past*. Because the past has already happened, we know what it looks like. The second piece of the puzzle is *the present*. Because the present is in front of us now, we know what it looks like. But the third piece of the puzzle is always a mystery: it is *the future*. And 'who can tell man what will be after him under the sun?' (v. 12).

Now, here is the catch in this puzzle: until we know the design of the third piece, we cannot understand why the other pieces are patterned the way they are. Until we know the whole picture, we won't understand why there are lines, marks, notches and colours on the other pieces in quite the way there are. The incomprehensible mystery of the future leaves us unable to understand fully why things happen today as they do.

We are, therefore, never able fully to understand life today for one simple reason: we do not have knowledge of the future as only God does.

Let me try another illustration to make this point clearer.

Suppose you begin to notice that people around you are acting strangely. Your brother is spending lots of time in his room with the door closed. And he smiles at you whenever he comes out (that's odd!). Your sister is also unusually nice. Friends are rarely available when you want to see them. Everyone is acting strangely. Then, one night, you come home to a surprise party in your honour. Suddenly, it becomes clear what everyone was doing. The end explains the enigmas of the preceding weeks.

This is the sense in which Qohelet poses questions about the outcome of things. Life is full of enigmas. If we understood what God was doing, the puzzling twists and turns of life would all make sense. But we don't understand the ends to which God is moving this or that detail of the world, so we are never able to comprehend why things unfold as they do. That is the gist of Qohelet's opening lesson on the limits of human wisdom.

Qohelet begins this introduction with a declaration of God's absolute knowledge and our ignorance (v. 10). The phrase 'Whatever has come to be has already been named' is an acknowledgement that someone (God) has already determined everything that comes to pass. To 'name' something in this context is to assign its purpose. Everything that comes to pass has already been named (that is, assigned a purpose) by God.

In theology, we call this the doctrine of God's *decrees*. The *Westminster Shorter Catechism*, question 7, puts it this way: 'The decrees of God are, his eternal purpose, according to the counsel of his will, whereby, for his own glory, he hath foreordained whatsoever comes to pass.' Everything happens according to God's 'naming'. There is a purpose for everything, but we cannot figure it all out.

'Man ... is not able to dispute with one stronger than he' (v. 10), Qohelet adds. When we are troubled by the twists of life, we lack the wisdom to correct God. The biblical book of Job is an excellent example of Qohelet's point. Job's life took some devastating turns through illness, the loss of family members and other tragedies. He wanted to argue with God because he could not make sense of his sorrows. But who is wise enough to question God? We can complain to God and cry out for help and for understanding (as modelled in the Psalms). But, as Job confessed at the end of his book (Job 42:1–6), we ultimately must confess that God's reasons are beyond our grasp. We do not understand the ends towards which he is moving this or that thread of life. The more we try to dispute life's enigmas, the more we expose the shallowness of human wisdom: 'The more words, the more vanity, and what is the advantage to man?' (v. 11).

As with a three-piece puzzle with one piece missing, the chief reason why we cannot understand the events of life is because we do not know the outcome God has 'named' for them (v. 12).

Praise God, he has not left us completely in the dark about his purposes! Scripture does give us general insight into his plans. He has not revealed his specific purposes for each particular event in the life of each person or community, but he has revealed as much as is necessary for our faith and trust in him. And as we come to know that God is good through all that he has revealed of his purposes, we are able to rest in the assurance that our unexplained troubles also fit within his good decrees.

This is the lesson of wisdom's limitations as we begin the second half of Ecclesiastes' study on life's vanities (*hebel*). What good is human wisdom when we lack the final puzzle piece crucial for real understanding? We will learn in this second half of Qohelet's book that human wisdom truly is of great value, just as we learned in the previous half of the book that labour and its rewards truly are to be enjoyed. But neither labour's rewards nor wisdom's insights are able to provide us with a stable foundation for joy in life. Wisdom is good, but in this vain world it is much more limited than we like to admit.

The sorrow of wisdom (7:1–12)

In this passage, Qohelet strings together a series of proverbs. As we enter into Qohelet's examination of wisdom, we should not be surprised that he begins to speak in proverbs. Proverbs that express metaphors, word pictures and analogies are the language of wisdom in the Old Testament world. We will encounter many proverbs in the second half of Ecclesiastes.

There are close to a dozen distinct proverbs rattled off in sequence in these verses (vv. 1–12). Each of the proverbs in this passage stands alone as an independent saying. Qohelet probably did not create these proverbs, but he probably gathered them into this mini-collection. These may have been well-known proverbs of the day, but Qohelet assembles this particular selection in order to capture a specific lesson about wisdom. Together, these proverbs serve like the scattered dots of a dot-to-dot puzzle aligning around a coherent theme: the relationship between wisdom and sorrow. On the one hand, the end of everything (under the sun) is death; on the other hand, it is at a thing's end that it has reached its fullest experience of maturity. Thus, life presents this profound congruence between sorrow and wisdom. Those who would be wise will note that it is sorrow that brings wisdom.

The opening proverb (v. 1) lays the foundation on which the rest follow: 'A good name is better than precious ointment, and the day of death than the day of birth.' 'Precious ointment' is a symbol for pleasure. It refers to the perfume or cologne worn when dressing for a great feast in Old Testament times. Such ointment is both pleasant in itself and a symbol for all the pleasure of the banqueting life. 'Precious ointment' is a metaphor for ease and pleasure.

Precious ointment is contrasted with 'a good name'. This phrase refers to more than the label by which a person is called (such as 'Sam' or 'Fred'). 'Name' refers to a person's identity: his or her inner life and being. Qohelet is contrasting the inner life of a person (his or her name) with the outer pleasures of life (precious ointment). He is telling us that the nurture of one's soul (a good name) is more rewarding than pleasant attainments (precious ointment).

That truth is expanded in the second line of the proverb with a shocking comparison between death and birth (v. 1b). If it is true that a good name far surpasses precious ointment in value, then the day of death is more to be honoured than the day of birth. Here Qohelet introduces the enigmatic congruence between sorrow and wisdom in the world. Qohelet does not mean for us to desire death: the crowning benefit of wisdom (under the sun) is that 'wisdom preserves the life of him who has it' (v. 12). Qohelet is not praising death. He is commending a good name, even though it is on the day of death that one's soul reaches its zenith (at least with regard to life under the sun).[2] This reality captures a general principle: wisdom tends to be found in the sorrows of life more than in its pleasures.

Verses 2–6 unfold a series of proverbs that continue to develop this theme. Notice some of the vivid turns of phrase Qohelet employs.

'Sorrow is better than laughter,' he says in verse 3, 'for by sadness of face the heart is made glad.' Qohelet is not commending sorrow: he is pointing us towards gladness. But the passing grin of the face is nothing compared with the supreme joy of a gladdened heart. And it is often through heartaches that the heart is stretched, deepened, enlarged and equipped for true joy. Thus this ironic truth is held out to us, that it is often by sadness of face that the heart learns joy.

In verse 6 Qohelet writes, 'For as the crackling of thorns under a pot, so is the laughter of the fools …' The ancient Hebrews valued all kinds of wood that could be harvested for lumber and other foliage good for food or medicines. But thorn bushes were good neither for building nor for eating. Thorns were good for nothing, except to be used as kindling to start a fire for cooking. As the thorns burned, they crackled.

Qohelet's proverb compares the crackling of thorns to the cackling of fools. Neither lasts long, and neither has real value. The laughter of those living for a good time dissolves into nothing. Once again, Qohelet is not naysaying joy. He is exposing the emptiness of frivolous pleasures ('precious ointment') in order to exalt the deep, abiding joy of those who learn wisdom ('a good name'). Ironically, it is through sorrows that the gladness of wisdom is often improved.

My parents live on a few acres in Oklahoma with several fruit trees and grape vines in their yard. When I visit, my father often enlists my help in pruning the trees and vines. The first time I did it, I was hesitant to cut too much, but my father urged me onwards. We pruned so drastically, I thought for sure that the vines would die. I was wrong: they produced greater fruit the next season because of the pruning. Jesus uses the metaphor of pruned vines to describe his loving nurture of disciples through hardships (John 15:1–11). Jesus says that such pruning comes 'that my joy may be in you, and that your joy may be full' (15:11). Jesus' lesson in John 15 is the same as the lesson of Qohelet in the present passage. Ecclesiastes does not commend nihilism or a fascination with misery. Instead, Qohelet calls us to the deep abiding joy that blooms from wisdom, even though wisdom typically grows in the soil of hardship.

In verses 7–10, Qohelet turns to a series of exhortations. Each of these proverbs gives an instruction for a noble response in times of strain. Verse 7 is an exhortation to honesty in times of oppression (not accepting bribes from the powerful). Verse 8 is an exhortation to patient humility in times of long waiting (not seeking the quick way to burnish one's name). Verse 9 is an exhortation to tolerance in times of conflict (not allowing offences to breed bitterness). Verse 10 is an exhortation to contentment in times of social decline (not pining after a past 'golden age'). These are the qualities that nurture wisdom in the midst of trouble. Hardships do not automatically produce wisdom; we must respond to suffering properly if we would profit by it. One must weather the storm faithfully to experience its joyful fruits of wisdom (cf. James 1:2–18). Qohelet's string of exhortations showcases the kinds of virtues that nurture wisdom in the midst of sorrows: honesty, patience, tolerance and contentment.

Verse 8 is a good example of these exhortations: 'Better is the end of a thing than its beginning, and the patient in spirit is better than the proud in spirit.' When constructing a great building, the builder typically starts with a set of blueprints and concept pictures. One might feel pride looking over lofty plans, but possessing the finished product is far better than looking over plans. It is through patience and much suffering that the better end is achieved. Therefore, patience is a quality that rewards with maturity and wisdom, but pride undermines it. 'It is better for a man to be patient until the end,' Robert Gordis remarks, 'than to be conceited at the beginning of an undertaking.'[3]

This section ends with praising the wisdom gained through a wholesome response to hardships. 'Wisdom is good with an inheritance, an advantage to those who see the sun. For the protection of wisdom is like the protection of money, and the advantage of knowledge is that wisdom preserves the life of him who has it' (vv. 11–12). Gaining materially ('an inheritance') is good, but it is *wisdom* that preserves life. Therefore, Qohelet extols the inheritance of wisdom as greater than the inheritance of wealth. Wisdom provides the security and peace that many expect silver to provide.

In this string of proverbs, Qohelet is commending the value of wisdom. We lack access to the big picture of what God is doing in the world, so our wisdom is always limited. Furthermore, the wisdom we do acquire often comes with sorrow. These are tragedies and limitations that sadden us. These are aspects of wisdom's vanities in this life under the sun. Notwithstanding these limitations, wisdom is immensely valuable and worth the quest. Wisdom is far superior to the crackling thorns of foolish pleasures.

The comfort of faith (7:13–18)

In these verses, Qohelet lifts our eyes back to the sovereignty of God. It is the call to trust that God is sovereign (that is, to fear the Lord) that repeatedly emerges in Ecclesiastes as the only solid foundation for joy in life's vanities. Having introduced the limited value of wisdom, Qohelet calls us to keep our quest to understand grounded in faith.

At the beginning of this passage, Qohelet brings our attention back to the 'Stronger One' (6:10) who 'names' (that is, assigns purpose) to everything that occurs: 'Consider the work of God: who can make straight what he has made crooked?' (7:13). To 'consider the work of God' (v. 13) is to acknowledge the fact that God is sovereignly at work, and that his work even advances in the broken ('crooked') events of life. Even this tangle now upon us finds its meaning—whatever it is—within the work of God. No one can (or should desire to) resist what he is doing (cf. Job 38—42). This is not a call to cease labouring for good and repairing what we can; it is an exhortation to trust God when the waters are over our head.

God is infinitely wise and sovereign. Not only does he see the whole picture, but also he is the one who appoints all that comes to pass. It is the 'crooked' things Qohelet specifically calls us to acknowledge as belonging to God's work. God makes many straight and good things, but it is in those 'crooked' turns in life that we need faith in God's sovereignty.

Qohelet drives home this lesson with two examples in verses 15–18: the one who is 'overly righteous' and perishes because of his excessive righteous-doing; and the one who is 'over-wicked', perishing in his sinful indulgences. Both extremes result from a failure to grasp God's sovereignty over the crooked circumstances of life.

Let me focus first on this 'overly righteous' person who wastes himself away in all his righteous-doing: 'There is a righteous man who perishes in his righteousness … Be not overly righteous, and do not make yourself too wise. Why should you destroy yourself?' (vv. 15–16). Many make the mistake of reading this passage as a warning against striving too hard to be holy (as though it were possible to be too holy!). For example, one commentator writes,

> Koheleth now urges the doctrine of the 'golden mean', ... [a] characteristic idea of Greek philosophy ... doubtless familiar to Koheleth ... Righteousness ... must not be pursued too zealously (v. 16). On the other hand, he cannot recommend the opposite practices of 'wickedness' and 'folly' either (v. 17) ... What is therefore best is a moderate course between both extremes (v. 18).[4]

This sounds like a Goldilocks approach to life: not too hot and not too cold, just lukewarm holiness. Perhaps the Greek philosophers promoted 'golden mean' moderation between piety and indulgence.[5] But none of the biblical prophets ever urged anyone not to take righteousness too seriously; and there is nowhere else in Ecclesiastes where we are taught to live a mediocre morality. It is a mistake to interpret this passage as a warning against *becoming* 'over-righteous'. Rather, it is a warning not *to do* too much in the name of righteousness. An 'over-righteous' person is someone who takes it upon him- or herself to correct every lie, to champion every cause, and to confront every evil he or she encounters in order to bring righteousness to a broken society.

When we forget that God is sovereign over all things—including the 'crooked' ones—we can develop an overwhelming drive to figure out and fix everything wrong about society. When we lose confidence in God's sovereignty, we begin to fear that society's wickedness is hindering God's work. We feel that God needs us to act before his good purposes can move forward. We take upon ourselves the burden to figure it all out (being 'overly wise') and to fix it all (being 'over-righteous'). Taking the burden to save the world upon our own shoulders will, indeed, destroy us (v. 16); and it is a consequence of neglecting the doctrine of God's sovereignty. Qohelet places no limits on our growth in righteousness, but he does call us to recognize that we have limits in what we can do to make the world right.

Likewise, Qohelet's instruction to avoid 'over-wickedness' is not to be read as an invitation to dabble in just a little bit of wickedness. *All* wickedness and folly are to be restrained. But when we lose sight of God's sovereignty over even the crooked things of life, we may conclude that God has lost control, so the struggle is not worth it. We surrender to worldly indulgence when we lose confidence that God is governing over the world. 'Over-wickedness' (or total indulgence) is the other extreme brought by a lack of confidence in God's sovereignty. Ironically, both an 'over-righteous' and an 'overly wicked' approach to the world lead to death. And both are rooted in ignorance of God's sovereignty.

Human wisdom is limited, but it is valuable. Through right responses to the hardships of life, our wisdom (and its joyful fruits) will increase. But it takes faith in God to respond rightly to difficulty. Ultimately, our wisdom is not found in figuring everything out; our wisdom is found in trusting that there is a wise God who is superintending this enigmatic world. It is the fear of the Lord that leads to wisdom.

'It is good', the text concludes, 'that you should take hold of this [i.e. the instruction not to be 'overly righteous'], and from that [i.e. the instruction not to be 'overly wicked'] withhold not your hand, for the one who fears God shall come out from both of them' (v. 18). It is in the fear of the Lord—not in labour's rewards nor in understanding—that the man or woman of God is secure.

Joy by faith

The Bible is full of stories of saints who suffered. Joseph suffered the oppression of his brothers and then the oppression of Egyptian slavery. Finally, Joseph was exalted to a position of blessing. Sarah suffered the anguish of barrenness despite her great longing for a child. Then God worked mightily to grant her a son in old age. Moses, David, Esther, Paul, and many other figures of Bible history suffered long before receiving the blessings God had been preparing all along.

It is important to understand that such accounts in the Bible are not given to teach that every hard story has a happy ending (under the sun). The Bible does not guarantee that every valley of darkness will end with a point of understanding and light (under the sun). Not every Hebrew enslaved in Egypt eventually became a prince in the land as Joseph did. Examples like that of Joseph are given to assure us that God sovereignly works his great good in all our trials, and glorious endings like Joseph's assure us that we can trust God whether or not our own troubles come to make sense within our lifetimes. We *can* trust him whose hand is sovereign and good, even when we cannot understand why life takes confusing turns.[6]

That is the lesson of faith despite the unsolvable enigmas of life. It is the lesson Qohelet is teaching us with delicate balance. He is, on the one hand, urging us to value wisdom; and he is, on the other hand, urging us not to place confidence in wisdom. Rather, place your confidence in the Lord.

This initial study of wisdom's value and vanity continues in the next chapter, where Qohelet further expands this lesson (7:19–8:14) and brings us to the port of joy (8:15).

Notes

1 In the modern world, we make a sharp distinction between natural causes and supernatural causes. In the ancient world, nature and supernature would not have been so sharply distinguished.

2 Notice that Qohelet contrasts the *day* of death with the *day* of birth. It is not death itself that is superior to birth. Cf. Sirach 11:28, 'Call no one happy before his death; by how he ends, a person becomes known' (NRSV).

3 Gordis, *Koheleth*, p. 262.

4 Ibid., pp. 265–266.

5 E.g. Aristotle, *Nicomachean Ethics*, 2.6–7. The modern movie *Eat, Pray, Love* (2010) is a popular contemporary version of this 'golden mean' approach to life.

6 This is the message of Hebrews 11, where we are introduced to a list of men and women who suffered in faith without receiving reward in their lifetimes, yet who lived rejoicing in God's promises.

Wisdom and the city: the vanity and value of wisdom II (7:19–8:15)

T he discovery of penicillin was one of the most world-changing developments of the last century. When Sir Alexander Fleming made the observations in 1928 that led to the development of penicillin, a whole new field of medicine was born: antibiotics. The medical world was rightly enthusiastic about the potential of antibiotics to fight disease. And in the decades since, countless more antibiotics have been discovered, bringing inexpressible benefit to humankind.

The invention of antibiotics has not eradicated disease completely. Modern society still suffers from diseases and infections. Penicillin was not a 'cure all', even though some early enthusiasts naively thought that antibiotics would bring an end to disease as we know it. That was not to be. And today, medical experts are increasingly aware of the great limitations of antibiotics.

In a similar way, human wisdom will never provide a 'cure all' for human dilemmas. Wisdom will always be hindered by the world's vanities. But just as no hospital would want to be without antibiotics, so none of us should abandon our desire for wisdom. Wisdom is vain (*hebel*); nonetheless, it is of inestimable value to those who acquire it.

In the previous study (6:10–7:18), Qohelet cautioned us to establish our hearts in the fear of the Lord and not to expect too much from wisdom. As we pick up the remainder of this section (7:19–8:15), Qohelet shows us the benefits of wisdom for society as an encouragement nevertheless to pursue wisdom. This extensive study on wisdom's vanity and value closes with another word of joy at the end of the present passage (8:15).

Wisdom and society (7:19)

'Wisdom gives strength to the wise man more than ten rulers who are in a city.' This verse introduces the benefit wisdom brings to society. The 'ten rulers' in this verse are a figure of speech for the city elders—the community government.[1] They are the ones who are the leaders and shapers of society. Yet one citizen with wisdom brings more strength to the community than all of those in positions of authority. It is clear that Qohelet intends to inspire his readers to pursue wisdom regardless of their social status, and to bring that strength to their communities.

With this simple thesis statement, Qohelet begins a survey of benefits that wisdom brings to society. In what follows, Qohelet will lead us through three snapshots of wisdom applied to life in the community. First, he gives a snapshot of the wise man's response to his subordinates (7:20–22). Lastly, he will give a snapshot of wisdom before one's superiors (8:1–9). In between these poles of social power, Qohelet teaches us a wise response to the dangers of sexual immorality (7:23–29).

Patience with inferiors (7:20–22)

This first snapshot is about gossip—the overheard grumblings of subordinates. As with many proverbs, the topic stated is probably meant to represent much more. Even though the stated topic is gossip, it represents the broader idea of disrespect among subordinates for their superior.

It is, of course, a superior's job to oversee those under his or her charge and to 'keep them in line'. Qohelet's proverb reminds us that a wise leader exercises that oversight with grace. He is not endorsing lax leadership, nor excusing disrespect among subordinates. This proverb about overlooking disrespect is not a cancellation of the fifth commandment and the biblical demand that authority be respected. But within the inflexible law of righteousness that authority should be honoured, wisdom will temper the way a leader manages disrespect.

The foundation of Qohelet's call for moderation is the leader's self-awareness: 'there is not a righteous man on earth who does good and never sins' (v. 20). With a sense of his own fallibility, a leader will not go out of his way to try to root out the errors of his subordinates. 'Do not take to heart all the things that people say' (v. 21a) probably means, 'Don't try too hard to find the faults in what others are saying about you.' If you listen too closely, you will probably find plenty: 'you hear your servant cursing you' (v. 21b). Rest assured, someone out there is speaking critically about you. But don't fret about it. And don't try too hard to dig it out.

When you do learn about critical gossip, the remainder of Qohelet's instruction kicks in: 'Your heart knows that many times you yourself have cursed others' (v. 22). Such instruction should not be read as a licence for those under authority to mock their leaders. Qohelet nowhere condones such cursing. He simply admits that it happens—and that you yourself have done it. By God's grace, the wise man will understand his own sinful lips and show tolerance when others speak sinfully against him.

This is wisdom: learning how to uphold righteousness with a sensible understanding of the vanities and realities of life that have to be negotiated. The wise man will learn to uphold respect for authority with the moderation taught by experience. Such wisdom exercised in leadership strengthens the community.

Moral fidelity (7:23–29)

When social commentators discuss the critical factors for healthy cities, they typically talk about issues such as economics, education, crime, business and politics. These issues are important threads in the fabric of society; but among all the cords woven together to form a human society, Qohelet tugs at this strand as of particular importance: sexual purity. The book of Proverbs likewise opens with warnings about the immoral woman (Prov. 2:16–19) and closes with praise of the virtuous wife (Prov. 31). Today's sociologists vary on what they regard as the most essential strand of social integrity, but Israel's king obviously places great stress on sexual purity for the integrity of his community.

Twice in the present passage Qohelet says that his emphasis on sexual purity comes after his examination of all aspects of society. First, in verses 23–25, he speaks of his endeavour to understand all facets of the city. His goal was to discern 'the scheme of things' (v. 25): that is, he sought to explore all the forces and issues that shape a society, to provide a wise man's accounting of the whole system. But Qohelet is modest in his conclusions. He admits that a full accounting is not humanly possible. Nevertheless, he offers this one important finding from his examinations: the importance of sexual purity for social cohesion (v. 26).

A second time, in verses 27–28, Qohelet reminds us that he sought to untangle the whole system that constitutes a community ('adding one thing to another to find the scheme of things'), but a full accounting is humanly impossible. Yet this one finding he (again) presents: the importance of moral fidelity (vv. 28–29).

Even though it is impossible fully to map the many forces that strengthen or weaken the web of relationships that constitute society, this topic is central to the integrity of the whole system. Sexual corruption is not a peripheral matter to the strength of a city, nor is it the obsolete fascination of prudish clericalism. Qohelet identifies sexual fidelity as central to a community's strength, and sexual immorality as more devastating to a land than death itself (v. 26).

The secret to overcoming sexual temptation is not will power nor prudish rules (though prudent rules have a place). The wise response to temptation promoted in this passage is to seek God's favour: 'He who pleases God escapes her' (v. 26). This is not a call to earn God's favour; it is a call to enter into God's favour through worship. Those who walk in his grace are strengthened against the temptations of the world. There is no programme of 'six steps to overcome temptation' here. Rather, this is a simple admission of human weakness and the need to throw oneself upon God's grace. Solomon gives further exhortations on the fear of the Lord and escaping sexual temptation in the book of Proverbs (esp. Prov. 5–7), but this is a great little summary of that lesson.

Qohelet's lesson on fidelity closes with a striking valuation: 'Behold, this is what I found, says the Preacher, while adding one thing to another to find the scheme of things … One man among a thousand I found, but a woman among all these I have not found' (vv. 27–28). These are not literal mathematical findings. Qohelet is expressing the immense value of uprightness in men—and especially among women—for the defence of moral purity in society. This comment on the rarity of godly women is another way of expressing the idea captured in Proverbs 31: 'An excellent wife who can find? She is far more precious than jewels' (Prov. 31:10). Godly men, and especially godly women, are of great importance for the moral integrity of a society.

It is no coincidence that Solomon's third wisdom book—the Song of Songs—is devoted to the topic of marital fidelity. In the Song of Songs, Solomon provides God's people with the ultimate romantic poetry extolling the power of sexual love to destroy or strengthen a society. The conclusion stated here in Ecclesiastes echoes the theme of the Song of Songs: 'Love is strong as death, jealousy is fierce as the grave' (S. of S. 8:6b; cf. Eccles. 7:26).[2]

After examining 'the scheme of things' that constitute a strong society, Qohelet identifies wisdom in matters of sexuality as of chief importance. It should not surprise us when people attempt to rewrite the social calculus in a manner that denies that sexual fidelity is such a big deal: 'See, this alone I found, that God made man upright, but they have sought out many schemes' (v. 29). It is a penchant of humanity to attempt to change the rules by which society can be woven together. Our own communities today are no exception.

Patience under authority (8:1–9)

The final snapshot in this series is the seat of government—the throne of the king, to be more specific. We don't have absolute monarchs in the modern West, and frankly some of the particulars in this passage apply only to the Old Testament monarchy. Not all the points of this passage apply directly to a modern democracy, but the principles remain instructive.

This passage opens with a generic proverb about the value of wisdom. Wisdom is rare and greatly to be prized. It brings joy to the one who attains it: 'his face [will] shine, and the hardness of his face is changed' (v. 1). A shining face is an expression of joy, and a softened face is the image of gentleness and peace. This praise of wisdom applies to all realms of life, but in this passage Qohelet applies it to service in the king's court.

Verses 2–9 counsel the wise man (with shining face and softened demeanour) to tread very carefully when in disagreement with the king. He urges the wise to obey the king's command out of a fear of the Lord (v. 2). He further exhorts us not to desert the king too quickly nor to join ourselves to his opposition too hastily. (That is the likely meaning of v. 3: 'Be not hasty to go from his presence. Do not take your stand in an evil [or contrary] cause.') To bite one's tongue and serve a king when you disagree with him requires the kind of confidence and peace verse 1 tells us comes with wisdom. Qohelet's counsel is not for absolute silence, but for wisely-timed appeals.

Obedience secures the king's favour ('Whoever keeps [the king's] command will know no evil thing [i.e. no penalty from the king]', v. 5). Meanwhile, 'the wise heart will know the proper time and the just way [to address the king]. For there is a time and a way for everything, although man's trouble lies heavy on him' (vv. 5–6).

The story of Nehemiah offers an illustration of a wise appeal. Nehemiah served the king of Persia, and with prayer and care he brought his appeal on behalf of Jerusalem (Neh. 2). Esther is another excellent example. She fasted and prayed for three days, then presented herself to the king with a carefully prepared appeal that she unfolded patiently over several banquets (Esth. 4–6).

Wisdom is not arrogant. Just as a wise man *in* a position of authority is not hasty to listen out for criticism from inferiors (7:20–22), so a wise man *under* authority is not hasty to bring correction to his superiors. Wisdom does not brashly overstep one's rank to correct an authority figure. Wise counsel is brought with wise words in wise timing. Qohelet is teaching us the nature of modest wisdom in response to authority. Such wisdom under authority will strengthen a society.

Let me note some of the particulars of Old Testament kingship in this passage that do not apply directly to a modern democracy, although the principles are relevant. The particular force of Qohelet's argument—'Keep the king's command, *because of God's oath to him*' (v. 2, emphasis added)—is unique to Old Testament Israel. The kings of Israel ruled under a covenant with God (cf. 1 Sam. 10:1; 16:12–14; Ps. 2:6–7). Even when King Saul had grown proud and evil, David refused to lay a hand against him because he was 'the LORD's anointed' (e.g. 1 Sam. 24:6). As Paul teaches in Romans 13:1–8, all government authorities rule at God's command and answer to him, but only Old Testament Israel's king ruled under an oath from God (cf. Ps. 89:3–4, 19–37). This is one distinction between Qohelet's example and the modern world.

A second distinction is related. In a modern democracy, civil rulers serve at the appointment of the people and are under covenant with the public (e.g. the preamble of the United States Constitution). In a modern democracy, there is a human voice that can hold a ruler accountable, asking, 'What are you doing?' (v. 4). In modern democracies, the general public does have the right openly to oppose their rulers and hold them to account in a manner not imaginable in ancient monarchies. In the Old Testament, it was God himself (often through prophets) who called kings to account. Old Testament kings were not 'above the law', but neither were they answerable to the general public. These particulars of Qohelet's example do not apply in a modern democracy. But the principle he teaches is universal for all kinds of government—and, for that matter, management—settings.

Wisdom is often found among inferiors, but the possession of wisdom does not license a person to speak down to his authorities. A wise person honours authority and seeks to offer his counsel in a manner that upholds that authority. Even though troubles weigh heavily upon his heart (v. 6), he will not allow those strains to undermine his propriety before the ruler.

Four proverbs conclude this paragraph (vv. 7–8). They are proverbs that humble us in our counsel to authorities. The first three remind us that no wisdom of man is ever certain. No man knows for certain what the outcome of matters will be (v. 7). No man has the power, ultimately, to avoid death (v. 8a). Once a war is undertaken, one cannot take a break nor turn back (v. 8b). These three proverbs capture the limits of wisdom and call us to be measured in our appeals to rulers. Then the fourth proverb pierces to the heart with a final warning: 'nor will wickedness deliver those who are given to it' (v. 8c). This final maxim cuts both ways. It warns us not to use wicked devices to counter an authority, for wickedness is never a right means for working salvation. It also assures us that, when a ruler is wicked, there will be an end to that wickedness (cf. v. 12). These are lessons that Qohelet learned from his reflections on the operations of government ('when man had power over man to his hurt', v. 9).

These three snapshots—wisdom with subordinates (7:20–22), wisdom in social relationships (7:23–29) and wisdom with superiors (8:1–9)—capture the point introduced in Ecclesiastes 7:19: wisdom strengthens societies.

Call to joy (8:10–15)

At the close of this section, Qohelet gives us a final snapshot: a scene at the graveyard. It should be obvious by now that the graveyard is a frequent classroom of Ecclesiastes. This is certainly not due to any delight in death; rather, it is death that unavoidably captures the inequities and unfairnesses of life. If we are to find a source of joy that is going to have any real value, it must be a source of joy that can face even the grave with peace.

At the conclusion of Qohelet's first lesson on the vanities of wisdom, he brings us back to the graveyard (vv. 10–14) and commends to us joy in the fear of God (v. 15).

Verse 10 describes the burial of a wicked man who was honoured in society. He imagines a community leader who went in and out of the temple all his life, approved by all around him, and who was buried with full honours. This is one of the absurdities of life—that the wicked get away with their wickedness and are honoured both in life and in death. It ought not to be so. But it happens.

Michael Fox argues for a different translation of verse 10 that, if correct, makes the absurdity even more stark. According to Fox, the verse reads, 'And then I saw the wicked brought to the grave, and they proceeded from the holy place, while those who had acted honestly were neglected in the city.'[3] In this reading of the verse, a burial procession for the wicked is described, carrying him in honour from the temple to his grave outside the city (cf. Job 21:32). On the other hand, 'those who had acted honestly' are left on the streets, neglected, when they perish. 'This is not to say that the bodies of the [righteous] dead are left within the city forever, but rather that immediately after their death, when they should be buried [in honour], they lie in neglect, while the wicked receive obsequies and are brought in procession from the city to the cemetery outside the walls.'[4]

Whether verse 10 focuses solely on the honoured burial of the wicked (the ESV translation), or contrasts the honoured burial of the wicked with the neglect of the honest man's corpse (per Fox), the basic point is the same: people do not receive what they deserve in this present vain world (under the sun). This is a basic theme of Ecclesiastes. 'This also is vanity' (three times, in vv. 10, 14).

In this instance, Qohelet lays blame for this inequity at the feet of a community's rulers. 'Because the sentence against an evil deed is not executed speedily, the heart of the children of man is fully set to do evil' (v. 11). Old Testament law contained two categories of law: moral or judicial laws that defined absolute holiness; and ritual laws that promised atonement for those who repented. To call for 'the sentence against an evil deed [to be] executed speedily' is not to call for Draconian penalties without room for mercy. God's laws for his people are full of provisions for mercy and forgiveness. But through punishment or through atonement, justice must be satisfied and 'sentence against an evil deed ... executed speedily'.

Qohelet observes that a society's failure to uphold such justice against evil confirms the sin already in men's hearts. Just as placing soft clay in a hot kiln will 'fully set' the clay in its shape, so 'the heart of the children of man is fully set to do evil' when community leaders fail to uphold righteousness. The passage is teaching us that wisdom in society is of great importance. Wisdom within community, and within the seats of leadership, will bring honour and blessing to a land. Nevertheless, we need not anchor our joy to the success of wisdom in our land. For even if the whole city collapses in folly and injustice, the fear of the Lord grants us solid reasons to rejoice.

'Though a sinner does evil a hundred times and prolongs his life, yet I know that it will be well with those who fear God, because they fear before him. But it will not be well with the wicked, neither will he prolong his days like a shadow, because he does not fear before God' (vv. 12–13). On what basis does Qohelet make such a confident assertion? There is no proof to be offered under the sun. As Ecclesiastes has admitted over and over, within the scope of this life the wicked often prosper without consequence. Yet we know that God is good. He is holy and just. Therefore, even if we cannot see evidence of perfect justice in this life, we know that somehow and in some way God will make all things right. Those who fear him will be rewarded. The fear of the Lord, alone, grants absolute certainty in the enigmas of human society. This alone grants a robust foundation for joy. 'And I commend joy, for man has no good thing under the sun but to eat and drink and be joyful, for this [joy] will go with him in his toil through the days of his life that God has given him under the sun' (v. 15).

There is a world-famous children's hospital not far from my home. You don't have to spend much time there to appreciate the great blessing modern medicine offers to the afflicted. At the same time, you don't have to spend long in any hospital to realize how limited medicine is. There is much human suffering modern medicine has no idea how to resolve. The human body is simply too complex, and each individual too unique, for even the most advanced medical researchers to understand fully how diseases can be treated. Notwithstanding these limitations on medical understanding, the understanding doctors and nurses can provide is extremely valuable for human life and happiness.

In a similar way, all human wisdom is severely limited and always will be; but that does not negate its great value. In the passages explored in this chapter, Qohelet has been urging us to pursue wisdom and to esteem its benefits for building a strong society. But our joy is not found in building a wise society. Our joy is in the fear of God, whose kingdom will be consummated in final justice and mercy.

Chapter 9

Notes

1 Gordis, *Koheleth*, p. 279. Cf. Ruth 4:2.
2 It has become popular in some modern treatments of Song of Songs to imagine illicit sexual scenarios into the text. Such readings probably say more about the sexual ideals of modern society than about the Song of Songs. The high view of marriage throughout the book (e.g. 2:4; 3:6–11) and the commitment to faithfully holding a single lover in explicit contrast to the multiplicity of sexual partners sought by others, including Solomon's own failure with many women which is openly critiqued in the book (e.g. 5:5–9; 6:3, 8–9; 8:11–12), give every reason to understand Song of Songs as upholding the same praise of sexual fidelity within marriage as the other Solomonic wisdom books and the rest of the Scriptures.
3 Fox, *A Time to Tear Down*, p. 282.
4 Ibid., p. 284.

Worship: the uncertainty of God's work and the certainty of God's love (8:16–9:10)

A n old book caught my eye on the library shelf, so I gently slid it into my hand. The author's name was John Quincy Adams (not the American president by that name), and the title across its front read *His Apocalypse: Wherein Is Set Forth a Detailed Panorama of the Prophetic Wonders of Daniel and Revelation.*[1] It was a book about the end times, published in the 1920s.

As I leafed through its pages with curiosity, the author laid out his case for a coded timeline of events up to the end of the world, discerned from the books of Daniel and Revelation. Rev. Adams also believed he had identified the dates for each event. He wrote that there would be a war in heaven from 3–11 April 1925. He wrote that Jesus would rapture the church out of the world on the last day of that war: 11 April 1925. (The book was first published in 1924.)

Furthermore, after the rapture, the world would enter a 2,375-day tribulation. Mustafa Kamal Atatürk, who had founded the modern nation of Turkey just a few years before, would take over the world and rule as Antichrist. Then, on 11 October 1931, Jesus would return for the final judgement and the end of all history. As I turned through more pages, I found words of exhortation inscribed for any reader who might stumble upon the book after Rev. Adams (and the rest of the church) had been raptured in 1925.

Sadly, many have made the mistake of attempting to read the countdown and final events of the world in the pages of Revelation. Such efforts have always brought disappointment (and have overlooked Jesus' warning in Mark 13:32). There is enough that God has revealed to us in the Bible to give us plenty to study and obey, but there is also a lot he has not revealed that we are not supposed to try to figure out (cf. Deut. 29:29; Rom. 11:33–34).

In this next section of Ecclesiastes, Qohelet gives us warning and encouragement in our desire to understand what God is doing in the world. He does not talk about end-times events, but the passage does warn us about those who 'claim to know … [but] cannot find … out' (v. 17). There are limits to what we can understand about God's work, but those limits need not hinder our joy as servants in his work. Furthermore, the limited nature of human wisdom should drive us to worship the God of unlimited wisdom.

Beyond comprehension (8:16–17)

These verses set the stage for the next section: humankind cannot figure out the work of God by wisdom. Even if one were to study day and night without sleep, it would not be possible to understand all God's work.

Have you ever been wrestling with a complex problem, striving to piece together countless details in an effort to make sense of them all? We get the sense Qohelet had 'applied [his] heart to know wisdom' (v. 16) with that kind of earnestness. When he speaks of one whose eyes receive no sleep night or day (v. 16b), he is probably describing himself. Daniel Fredericks translates the statement thus: 'As I devoted myself to know wisdom and to see the affliction that is inflicted on the earth, even though sleep is not seen in one's eyes day or night, still, I observed that one is unable to understand all God's work, the work [of God's] which is done under the sun' (vv. 16–17a).[2]

What is God doing in human history, and in the events of my own life? Scripture does teach us what God's general purposes are in all that he does. We can praise God for all that he *has* gloriously revealed to us in

Scripture about his heart and purposes. We are not left without understanding concerning the overarching works of God. But we are nowhere told what God is doing in the particulars of our lives. We cannot figure out why he weaves the specific events of our lives the way he does. 'Even though a wise man claims to know, he cannot find it out' (v. 17).

Some scholars suggest the final phrase of verse 17 should be translated differently. It should probably read, 'Even though a wise man *intends* to know, he cannot find it out.'[3] That is, wise men like King Solomon might try to discern the mind of God in the happenings of the world, but they can never succeed in that effort.

You might be able to figure out what your friends or family members are up to. But no one can comprehend what God is doing. I imagine that if Solomon were writing today, he might replace the image of a wise man sitting awake all night with that of a scientist running algorithms through a supercomputer around the clock. Crunching all the data to figure out God is simply not feasible.

Beyond knowing by events (9:1–6)

The previous discovery—that God's work cannot be figured out by wisdom—leads us to a startling conclusion. If even the wisest human being cannot discern the purposes of God by night-and-day study, then we cannot know (by our own wisdom) if God is pleased with us or angry at us.

'But all this I laid to heart, examining it all,' Qohelet begins this next passage. In other words, what follows are the author's ruminations after taking to heart the preceding observations. These are Qohelet's conclusions: 'those who are righteous and wise and their works are in God's hand. Yet, whether it is love or hatred a man cannot know, both are before him' (9:1–2, a.t.). Be sure to note the opening word of assurance here. It is a word of assurance we will need to cling onto, and it is a word of assurance we will return to later. Qohelet states with confidence this certainty: that those who are wise and righteous are in God's hand. He does not speak about the wicked being in God's hand, for this is not a statement about God's power over all, righteous and wicked alike. He is making a statement about God's special favour upon the righteous. They are in his hand.

Notwithstanding that certainty, Qohelet advances to his subsequent cry of alarm. Despite whatever confidence the righteous may have in God, no man can guess whether a day will bring an experience of love or of hatred. Both are just as likely.

Now, we must be careful here. At the end of this section, Qohelet will bring us back to words of assurance concerning God's favour upon the righteous. There *is* certainty of God's love in which his people rest. Qohelet launched us with that certainty (v. 1) and he will end by bringing us back to that certainty (v. 7). Nevertheless, he uses provocative language here to capture the futility of any human effort to guess the disposition of God based on one's experiences. Sometimes the righteous suffer in ways that seem downright hateful. But this does not mean that God is angry, punishing that person. Examining life 'under the sun' (8:17), we simply cannot draw conclusions from our experiences as to whether God's favour is upon us.

Sadly, there are many popular Christian authors and television preachers who promote a confused message about God's love. They say that we can tell whether God is happy with us by the material prosperity and health we have or don't have. Contrary to such teachings, Jesus said, '[God] makes his sun rise on the evil and on the good, and sends rain on the just and on the unjust' (Matt. 5:45). God is very patient. We must be patient, too. External experience is not a reliable gauge of God's favour or the lack thereof.

The ultimate proof of this point is the fact that both the righteous and the wicked alike face death (vv. 2–3). In fact, all manner of sorrows afflict both the righteous and the sinner alike. Death is just the extreme example.

Pointing to death is a metaphor for all manner of misfortune that blindly (it seems) falls upon rich and poor, high and low, young and old, good and bad alike.

This is not a new lesson; Qohelet has made this point before. But this time, Qohelet speaks particularly about *the worshipper of God* receiving the same sorrows as the wicked. In verse 2, the contrasts are all terms of Old Testament worship: '... the same event happens to the *righteous* and the *wicked*, to the *good* and the *evil*, to the *clean* and the *unclean*, to *him who sacrifices* and *him who does not sacrifice*. As the *good one* is, so is the *sinner*, and *he who swears* is as *he who shuns an oath*' (emphasis added). Qohelet is not just contrasting the nice with the bad: he is specifically contrasting the faithful worshipper of God with the one who denies God. The expressions he uses all refer to states of piety, ritual purity and covenantal worship in an Old Testament context. Nevertheless, worship does not bring about guarantees of a better experience of life. Both the pious and the impious experience the same uncertainties of life under the sun.

It should not be this way. After this string of contrasts, Qohelet laments, 'This is an evil [that is, a tragedy] in all that is done under the sun, that the same event happens to all' (v. 3). It is evidence that our world is broken that both the righteous worshipper and the godless experience similar results in God's world. It should not be this way. But it is.

As usual, Qohelet elaborates further on the vanity of all this. Perhaps he wants to be sure that we fully appreciate the problem. Or maybe he wants to assure us that he fully understands the problem!

> Also, the hearts of the children of man are full of evil. Indeed, folly is in their hearts as long as they live, and after that they go to the dead. For, to him who is joined with all the living there is hope (since for a living dog it is better than a dead lion), for the living know that they will die, but the dead know nothing and they have no more reward, since their memory is forgotten. Their love,

their hate, and their desire have already perished, and there is no more place for them in all that is done under the sun (vv. 3b–6, a.t.).

In this translation, I have endeavoured to bring out the flow of thought that seems to run through these verses. Rather than reading the passage as a sequence of disjointed remarks about evil hearts, living dogs, hope and lost desires, it is best to recognize a single idea developing through these verses. Qohelet is grieving the fact that men point to their mortality as a reason to pursue folly during their short lives. Instead of driving men to worship (as it ought), mortality becomes a licence to run after madness. 'Folly is in their hearts as long as they live, and after that they go to the dead' (v. 3b). The rest of this block of text (about dogs and lions, hope and so forth in vv. 4–6) captures the thinking by which men justify their folly. As long as they are still alive, men have hope of reward. Knowing that death is coming when their pursuits will end and they will have no more part in the rewards of the living, men are driven to make the most of life. This is the thinking that justifies a life of madness. It is better to be a dog (a creature of disdain) who is alive and has scraps to enjoy, than a lion (a creature of nobility) who is dead and no longer enjoys the hunt.

Ironically, Qohelet nowhere disagrees with any of these facts. Indeed, Qohelet's final words of encouragement in verse 10 will repeat the same basic point: that our part in the world concludes when we die. Qohelet does not discount any of these facts about life's brevity and death's finality. He does regard it as a tragedy, however, that such observations drive men to folly.

Under the sun, there are no grounds for ascribing benefit for faithfully worshipping God. But Qohelet does not end the matter there. There is a basis for the godly to know certainty in God's grace in a life of worship and righteousness.

Call to joy ... in God's approval (9:7–10)

Here are the only certain grounds for joy in life: *the approval of God* which is already assured to those who worship him (those reckoned as righteous).

It is important to read verse 7 in context. This is not a blanket statement of God's approval on everyone. As we earlier noted, Qohelet began this segment with the assertion that the righteous and their works 'are in the hand of God' (v. 1). He further focused attention on the fate of godly worshippers in contrast with the impious. Although there is no demonstrable difference in the quality of life experienced by the righteous compared with that of the wicked under the sun, the approval of God declared upon his people in worship is itself grounds for joy. That is the anchor Qohelet casts in verse 7.

The passage is calling us to a frank decision of faith, trusting that God is true to his word of grace regardless of the hardships of life. Rather than looking for experiential signs of God's approval, 'God has already approved what you do' (v. 7). The righteous and their works are already in his hand (v. 1).

The string of exhortations to joy that follow provide a cascade of celebratory themes. Eating and drinking (v. 7a) is Qohelet's regular metaphor for joy—here we are urged again to eat and drink 'with a merry heart'. White garments (v. 8a) are the garments of festal celebration. You don't wear white when going to work in the fields. In fact, most contemporaries of Qohelet probably did not own such attire. But the point is clear, whether or not a hearer could literally afford white robes.

Oil poured on the head (v. 8b) is another symbol of feasting and joy (cf. 7:1). The image of a luxurious abundance of oil ('Let not oil be lacking on your head') would, again, have been beyond the economic means of most hearers of this text in Old Testament times. Enjoying life with a woman you love 'all the days of your vain life' (v. 9) is a beautiful reminder that marriage is a gift from God. A spouse is to be a support and comfort through all the vanities of life. The Hebrew expression is quite touching; it speaks of marrying 'for love'. Qohelet has written this book with young people as his primary audience (cf. 11:9). Here, his encouragement to unmarried youth is to marry for love. It is not a call to 'follow your heart' in the modern sensual sense of the phrase; it is an encouragement to marry for that love which will bring comfort during the many vanities of life a couple will face together. 'The point is that a man should marry a woman he loves, not, say, one who only brings a hefty dowry or family connections.'[4]

This string of exhortations—to eat and drink, to don white robes, to pour much oil and to enjoy marital love—leads us through a parade of joyful celebrations. Most importantly of all, remember the reason for this sudden switch from the sombreness of previous paragraphs to this extravagant scene of rejoicing: this is a call to rejoice because the approval of God is upon those who worship him. Whatever hardships life throws at them, worshippers of God can still rejoice in the assurance of his favour.

Qohelet seals his list of celebratory enjoyments with this purpose statement: 'because *that* is your portion [or reward] in life and in your toil which you toil under the sun' (v. 9, emphasis added). The pronoun translated 'that' is singular, not plural. It would have to be plural ('these') if Qohelet meant us to regard the list of celebratory pleasures as the rewards of our toil. The pronoun is also masculine. It would have to be a feminine pronoun if Qohelet meant to identify the last item on his list—a loving wife—as the reward he has in view. Rather, the pronoun at the end of the paragraph points back to the heading of the whole list: the approval of God upon the righteous. It is the declaration of God's approval received in worship that is the one certain reward the worshipper enjoys in life. It is that one certain reward that gives reason to rejoice in whatever other good things we experience in life.

Qohelet is forcing us to do a spiritual backflip. Imagine someone taking you into a dark room, back to the very darkest corner, switching off all the lights, waiting until your eyes have completely adjusted to the pitch blackness, and then suddenly flipping on the brightest of all lights. Our text has led us to the dismal emptiness of life's uncertainties under the sun, then suddenly switched on the blinding light of God's grace that puts joy into everything which was otherwise tenuous and uncertain.

The last verse of the paragraph drives home the irony of Qohelet's call to joy. 'Whatever your hand finds to do, do it with your might, for there is no work or thought or knowledge or wisdom in Sheol, to which you are going' (v. 10).

Many commentators interpret verse 10 as indication that Qohelet did not believe in a resurrection afterlife. It is sometimes said that Qohelet believed that all the dead, the godly included, descended to a shadowy underworld existence devoid of meaningful thought or purpose. But this is not a dismal conclusion Qohelet announces. Notice how verse 10 employs the very terminology of under-the-sun despair earlier considered (cf. vv. 5–6). He is deliberately adopting the same facts cited earlier as the basis for mad living in order to turn those same facts on their head as suited to the motivation for righteous living. The same prospect of death that drives the wicked to mad folly will lead the worshipper, assured of God's grace, to rejoice and make the most of life (v. 10). Both conclusions share the same understanding that man makes no more contribution to the world after death. One perspective (folly under the sun) takes this as reason not to bother; the other (joy in God's grace through worship) takes this as reason to make the most of life under the sun while it lasts.

The phrase 'whatever your hand finds to do, do it with your might' is like saying, 'Take up the work that fits your hand and give it all you've got.' Each of us has unique gifts and unique opportunities. Somehow, in the convergence of our gifts and the opportunities we encounter, God calls us to 'find a suitable fit' and then devote our strength to it. Our opportunity to labour will soon come to an end. Worship God all through life, and let his grace provide the reason to enjoy your life (whatever its hardships) as you make the most of your days while they last.

Chapter 10

Notes

1 The full title was actually *His Apocalypse: Wherein Is Set Forth a Detailed Panorama of the Prophetic Wonders of Daniel and Revelation, Which Will Have Complete and Literal Fulfillment in the Final 2375 Days of This Age.*

2 Fredericks, 'Ecclesiastes', p. 200.

3 Delitzsch, *Commentary on The Song of Songs and Ecclesiastes*, p. 353; Fox, *Time to Tear Down*, p. 290.

4 Fox, *A Time to Tear Down*, p. 294.

Wisdom and folly: a portrait of modest wisdom (9:11–11:8)

G old has been prized throughout history. Its beauty and rarity make it the metal of kings and of gods. But gold is also a fragile metal. It is soft, which makes it easier to work into ornate pieces of jewellery, but also leaves it vulnerable to damage.

Wisdom is like gold. That is the theme of this final section of Qohelet's wisdom study. Not only is wisdom difficult to attain, but also it is difficult to maintain unspoiled by folly. The life of Solomon himself is a testament both to the greatness of wisdom and to its fragility in the face of human lusts and foolishness (e.g. 1 Kings 11:1–14).

In this closing section on the vanities of the quest for wisdom, Qohelet urges us to value this great aspiration like gold—with esteem, yet mindful of its weaknesses.

Wisdom's strength … and weakness (9:11–18)

The first two verses of this passage (vv. 11–12) caution against overconfidence in one's strengths. When running a race, speed is a good thing, but the fast do not always win. The fastest runner may sprain his ankle and lose. The mightiest soldier is as vulnerable to a stray bullet as any (e.g. 1 Kings 22:34). Sometimes it is the simplest start-up companies that capture the public imagination, while the big corporations with the most advanced research facilities struggle to survive.

Speed is an obvious benefit to a runner and does give an important advantage in a race. Likewise, strength and intelligence are definite assets to value. But these strengths are no guarantee: 'time and chance happen to them all' (v. 11). Just as the fish is unwittingly caught in a net, so all manner of unexpected obstacles—most notably death itself—can suddenly interfere with and change everything.

The phrase 'time and chance' is a Hebrew expression for chance happenings. Ultimately, God's sovereign decrees govern all things (recall the lesson of 3:1–15). From God's perspective, nothing is just due to chance. There is a mind and a purpose that rule the day. That conviction is a key principle undergirding the entire book of Ecclesiastes. Nevertheless, our inability to discern the mind of God in the twists and turns of life makes our experience of events seem to be characterized as random and chance.

The book of Ruth uses a similar expression to describe Ruth's 'happening' upon the field of Boaz while gleaning (Ruth 2:3). As the story of Ruth unfolds, we find that God's hand was actually guiding her steps all along. However, from the perspective of human experience, Ruth's stumbling upon the field of Boaz was a chance occurrence. Without denying the providence of God over all things, the Scriptures also affirm the randomness of life events as we experience them. Within our 'under the sun' (v. 11) experience of life, the turns of life are full of 'time and chance' events. However skilled we may be, the unexpected often trumps our efforts.

The point of this opening reflection on 'time and chance' is not to discourage skill. A strong arm and sturdy sword certainly do help in the day of battle! But Qohelet is teaching us circumspect modesty in our strengths. A healthy measure of scepticism ought to be maintained with regard to all human strengths, such as speed, power and intelligence. Nevertheless, it is the fragility of wisdom in particular that Qohelet wants to focus upon. Hence his introductory 'Again I saw … under the sun' remarks about all manner of traits (vv. 11–12) are followed by a more focused look at wisdom: 'I have also seen this example of wisdom under the sun …' (v. 13).

Wisdom is greater than the other traits already mentioned (speed, might and intelligence). That is the lesson advanced in Qohelet's story of the warrior king and the poor man in verses 13–16. Before showing us the fragility of wisdom, Qohelet first asserts the greatness of wisdom. It is not just another human strength like speed for a runner or might to a soldier. Wisdom is a superior benefit to humanity, one to be desired more greatly than the others. This story of the warrior king and the poor man illustrates the unique benefit of wisdom.

The significance of this story hinges on how we translate verse 15. Some translations give the impression that the citizens of the besieged city had sought the wisdom of the poor man when their troubles mounted. '*But there was found in it* a poor, wise man, and he by his wisdom delivered the city …' (v. 15). Some think this is the story of a known wise man who is looked to for help during a battle, but then afterwards is unappreciated. But the Hebrew literally says, 'He [that is, the attacking king] found in [the city] a man who was poor but wise …' The people of the city did not seek out this poor, wise man. They never knew what he had done.

The attacking king encountered a poor man of the city during his siege. Perhaps while his army was maintaining armaments outside a walled city, a poor man outside the city walls was captured and brought to the king for intelligence about the city. Then somehow, in the course of the king's interview with the man, the poor man persuaded the king to withdraw from the attack altogether. We do not know exactly how it happened, but somehow the king was persuaded to withdraw by a few wise words from an unknown poor man. Yet no one in the city ever knew about it, and for the rest of his days, that man's neighbours continued to brush him off as a poor beggar of no consequence. 'Yet no one remembered that poor man … the poor man's wisdom is despised and his words are not heard' (v. 15).

One wonders if Solomon is retelling a story of one of his father's battles, since David had been a great warrior king. Maybe David was the great king who recounted to Solomon the story of an attack he once abandoned on account of a single poor man's words. It is impossible to know where Solomon obtained this story, since the man was not remembered by his own people.

The point of Qohelet's little narrative is to illustrate the glory which people ascribe to might, yet the true superiority of wisdom even over power. People exalt the wealthy and the strong, heeding their words and ignoring the words of the poor and the weak. But wisdom is the greatest form of power above all the rest. Wisdom is even more powerful than royal might.

Qohelet's short story is setting us up. For, after exalting the superiority of wisdom, the writer now points our attention to something that will defeat even wisdom. It is folly that trumps both wisdom and power. 'Wisdom is better than weapons of war, but one sinner destroys much good' (v. 18). Wisdom is mightier than all else, but even wisdom is fragile. It takes only one foolish act to destroy a lifetime of wise labours. How many politicians, churchmen and other public figures can testify to that?

A portrait of wisdom begun (10:1–7)

By the late 1780s, Marie Antoinette was in a political crisis. French anti-royal sentiments were mounting. The extravagance of the queen in a time of national economic distress, combined with her rumoured involvement in recent scandals, fuelled opinions that would eventually lead to her beheading. In a desperate effort to avoid her public demise, Marie Antoinette commissioned a new portrait.

The portrait, which still hangs at the Palace of Versailles, presents Marie Antoinette seated with her children gathered around her, including an empty cradle representing a daughter who died in infancy.[1] In that day, royal portraits did not typically include children, but the flamboyant queen was attempting to present herself to the nation as a mother figure with family values. It is one of the great historic examples of political spin. It didn't work, and in 1792 the French monarchs were imprisoned and later beheaded.

Throughout history, portraits of the great have often been painted in order to flatter their subjects. Less attractive features would be downplayed or hidden altogether, and settings created to present the subject in the best possible light (as in the famous family portrait of Marie Antoinette). But Qohelet does no such thing in the portrait of wisdom that he gives to us in the present passage. Wisdom is of great nobility, but it is vulnerable to folly. That point has already been established. Now Qohelet leads us in a string of proverbs extolling the proper benefits of wisdom, yet mindful of its fragility. It is a portrait of wisdom that is honest about its weaknesses.

The first proverb compares wisdom to a perfumer's fine fragrance (v. 1). The perfumer carefully measures out his precious oils and spices, and heats them on his stove. But all his labours are ruined when a few flies, drawn by the sweet aroma, fall into the fragrance and turn the whole mixture into a stench. So the beauty of wisdom, so hard won, is quickly ruined by a moment of folly.

The second proverb is similar (v. 2): 'A wise man's heart inclines him to the right,' it begins. The right hand is traditionally the seat of honour. Wisdom leads to honour. 'But a fool's heart [inclines him] to the left,' the proverb ends. The force of the proverb is in the order of its presentation. Wisdom does bring honour, but the final word goes to folly and the dishonour that it brings. We should not read this proverb as though it describes two distinct individuals: one person who is always wise and tending towards honour, while the other is always foolish and dishonoured. This proverb sets contrasting figures before us to force us to wrestle with *both* dispositions in our own heart. It is wisdom that will incline towards honour; but when folly reigns in the heart, it leads to shame and ruin.

A third proverb similarly describes the shame brought by folly. Even as a fool walks down the street, his folly is obvious to all who watch him (v. 3). The word picture is one of imprudent impulsiveness. The fool is not literally 'say[ing] to everyone that he is a fool', but his ignorance of the sensible route to take makes it evident. This proverb about the fool's impulsiveness is followed by a proverb honouring a wise man's patience: 'If the anger of the ruler rises against you, do not leave your place, for calmness will lay great offences to rest' (v. 4). The ruler's rage here is so severe that the courtier is liable to lose his post, but the proverb assures us not to anticipate being removed, but rather to respond with the quality called *marpeʿ* in Hebrew. Translated 'tranquillity' or 'calmness', the word refers to that soothing spirit of patience that brings healing to what has been wounded (cf. Prov. 14:30; 15:4). Such patience is a skill that the wise will develop, in contrast with the impulsiveness that exposes a fool.

Each of these proverbs describes a different scene and its lesson. By stringing them together, Qohelet uses them like strokes of a paintbrush to create a portrait of wisdom. It is a portrait that shows wisdom's true beauty but also exposes wisdom's vulnerability to folly. In verses 5–7, Qohelet continues this message, bemoaning the damage caused when folly is given preference over wisdom.

His painting in verses 5–7 is one of general inversion: the rich are seated in low places while the fools are in high seats of honour; princes are walking while slaves ride on horses. Notice the only position given a value judgement in this picture is the one he names first: the high-seated *fools*. We are not told whether the rich are noble landowners or abusive elitists. We are not told whether the princes are corrupt and extravagant, or if they are honourable. We are probably meant to assume the best and proper character of each position he describes, except the one position he specifically marks as foolish. He is describing the inversion of the entire society that follows when folly is given influence in the land. That is why his picture starts with the placement of folly in high places, as 'an error proceeding from the ruler'. Once a ruler begins placing fools in high places, the result is the topsy-turvy undermining of everything else.

The portrait painted by this whole series of proverbs, showing both wisdom's importance and its fragility, is one we have only just begun, for another sixteen or so proverbs follow, filling out the image.

A portrait of wisdom continued (10:8–11:5)

A photomosaic is a large picture made out of many tiny pictures. One of the most popular is a photomosaic of Abraham Lincoln made by the inventor of the process, Robert Silvers.[2] From across the room, the picture looks like the face of the sixteenth president of the United States. As you step closer, however, it becomes clear that the portrait is formed out of hundreds of tiny photos from the American Civil War. Qohelet is doing something similar in Ecclesiastes 10:1–11:5. So far, we have examined five of Qohelet's maxims (vv. 1–7), but there is more. Viewed one by one, these proverbs jump abruptly from topic to topic; when they are considered together, however, a single theme emerges. Let us briefly survey the remaining proverbs in small sub-groups, one or two at a time. Then we'll step back to consider the big picture.

The next couple of proverbs (vv. 8–9) describe a series of dangers that accompanied certain vocational tasks of the day: digging a pit and falling in, breaking down walls and disturbing a snakes' nest, quarrying stones and being injured by rocks, or getting hurt while splitting logs. The point of the proverbs is this: when you have an area of skill, you are apt to do that thing more, and because you are doing it more, the likelihood you will be harmed in that pursuit increases. Thus, the ironic insight of these maxims is that your area of expertise is also most likely to be your area of demise.

In verses 10–11, two more proverbs that go together are quoted. These proverbs come from the worlds of the wood cutter and of the snake charmer. Each of them teaches us that wisdom is only beneficial when it is applied, and applied at the right time. Like an axe that cuts more effectively when sharpened, so one's efforts will be more effective if conducted wisely. On the other hand, a snake charmer may be skilled in calming serpents, but that skill does no good after the bite has occurred. Both of these maxims show us the lack of wisdom's value when not applied wisely.

A series of sayings about speech follows in verses 12–15. A wise man's words are valued and 'win him favour' (v. 12). But the words of a fool are too many, are rash, and though they begin in harmless chatter, they end with real and lasting damage (vv. 13–14). The final saying in this group does not explicitly mention speech, but it continues the same thought: 'The toil of a fool wearies him, for he does not know the way to the city' (v. 15). To 'not know the way to the city' is an idiom for being so eager to get started on a trip that one does not take time to get directions first. The modern equivalent is 'spinning one's wheels'. The toil of the fool who 'spins his wheels' will weary him and accomplish nothing.

In verses 16–17, Qohelet contrasts the condition of a nation with respect to the wisdom or immaturity of its king. The expression 'son of the nobility' does not refer to the king's lineage, but to his character. A 'son of the nobility' is one who bears the resemblance (that is, the character) of nobility. The only difference between the two scenes is the nobility or childishness of the king, but the result is spread through all the lower officers of the kingdom. The land is blessed when the ruler is wise, and not when he is foolish.

The proverb in verse 18 teaches us that inherited wisdom must be maintained with present wisdom. What past generations have built through great labour will not remain intact unless the current generation maintains it. The metaphor of a house is meant to stir our thoughts about a household and about a kingdom. Just as a roof and the house's walls will naturally deteriorate without care, so wisdom is essential in every generation. In ancient Israel, the flat roofs of houses were covered with lime, and this coating had to be regularly refreshed or else the roof would crack and leak.[3]

In verse 19, Qohelet follows the theme of feasting from previous verses with a proverb about bread and wine. As we have seen so often in Ecclesiastes, bread and wine are pictures of joy. But the twist at the end of this proverb reminds us that one cannot sit around and rejoice all day long. One has to labour to earn money with which to provide the food and wine. The force of the proverb is to commend celebration, but only if you are productive and have something to celebrate.

In verse 20, we return to the theme of speech with a proverb about guarding criticism. Even what is stated in secret is apt to become known in public. Qohelet uses the metaphor of a bird on the window sill broadcasting your secret mutterings. It is not that a bird would literally do this; it is a word picture for the surprise experienced when others learn what you thought no one heard. Nowadays, this proverb finds application among the surprising spread of private cellphone photos, emails or text messages. Expect that everything you say or write may one day be heard by others. The specific focus of the proverb is on cursing the powerful and being found out by them. The reason why the king and the wealthy are identified in this example is because there are obvious and frightful consequences if one is found cursing the influential (cf. Exod. 22:28). The example mentions rulers only to capture the lesson with a spirit of gravity, but its meaning is applicable to all speech.

The four proverbs grouped together at the start of chapter 11 are words of investment wisdom. These are ancient examples of financial advice. The first ('Cast your bread upon the waters …') advises long-term investments that will bring loss today but likely income in the future.

Often, this proverb is interpreted as an exhortation to generosity. For example, the medieval Jewish rabbi Samuel ben Meir interpreted this verse, 'Do a favor for a man from whom you never expect to benefit, because in the far future he will do a favor for you.'[4] Certainly, generosity is a good thing to encourage, but generosity is never to be encouraged based on the expectation of return. This saying urges us to 'cast forth bread' today for the specific purpose of expected return in the future. It cannot be a proverb about generosity. Instead, as confirmed by the connected proverbs in the subsequent verses, it is a maxim about investment. A log cast into the ocean current may be washed out to sea, but it will return with the tide on another day. Likewise, a wise steward is to find ways to invest his 'bread' for future returns. Purchasing a cow today that will provide calves and milk in the future is one example of 'casting bread upon the waters'. In those few instances where Hebrews had excess wealth, loaning money at interest for a business venture would be another example. Hebrews were prohibited from charging interest on loans that were given to the poor for survival needs (e.g. Lev. 25:35–37), but commercial loans still expected income. In these and other ways, this proverb urges present-day sacrifices in ways that will secure future provision.

The second verse presents a comparable word of financial advice. If verse 1 encouraged investment for the future, verse 2 encourages diversification to protect against total loss in case of a disaster. 'Give a portion to seven, or even to eight, for you know not what disaster may happen on earth' (v. 2). The equivalent saying today is, 'Don't put all your eggs into one basket.'

Verses 3–4 capture the unavoidable risks of all human labours, urging us not to let uncertainties hinder us from trying. The principle of uncertainty is captured in verse 3: 'If the clouds are full of rain, they empty themselves on the earth, and if a tree falls to the south or to the north, in the place where the tree falls, there it will lie.' The two images here are of provision (rainfall) and failure (a falling tree). Neither is under human control. In the understanding of ancient science, clouds gather water and then dump when they are full. We cannot control where or when that will happen. In like manner, when a tree falls, it is as likely to fall one way as the other. Once it does fall, that is where it will lie. A clever physics scholar or meteorology student might balk at these examples, rattling off all that modern science has uncovered about the nature of rainfall and falling objects. Modern science may enhance our ability to understand these phenomena so that these specific examples no longer convey the same degree of mystery they once did. Nevertheless, the principle they are cited to illustrate remains true: there is much behind human success and failure that is beyond human control.

The principle in verse 3 is applied in the proverb in verse 4: 'He who observes the wind will not sow, and he who regards the clouds will not reap.' Because rainfall and other forces can never be known with certainty, one who waits for certainty before planting will never gain anything. In other words, a measure of wisdom is helpful for guiding one's endeavours, but certainty is not possible.

The final proverb that concludes the series is unlike those that precede it: 'As you do not know the way the spirit comes to the bones in the womb of a woman with child, so you do not know the work of God who makes everything' (v. 5). This is the only proverb in this collection that has no application to human endeavour. It is the one proverb that lifts our eyes solely to the works of God, using the mystery of childbirth to remind us of the incomprehensibility of his works. How the body of a child forming in the womb becomes a distinct living being is a marvel that has long boggled philosophers and scientists. This is a strategically chosen proverb to complete the list. It reminds us that all of human life, including the receiving of life itself, is filled with mystery only understood by God.

So what is the big picture Qohelet wants us to see in this string of proverbs?

The sixteen or so proverbs in this sequence seem like a sampler plate. Rather than presenting us with a complete picture, they are like a sampler tray of desserts at a fine restaurant. They give us a taste of wisdom and whet our appetite for more. (We can turn to the book of Proverbs for a more complete collection of such wise sayings.) The author of Ecclesiastes clearly had an encyclopaedic knowledge of Hebrew proverbs, but he made a limited selection for this passage. The resulting collection here is scattered and disparate in its topics; nevertheless, there is a particular theme Qohelet has chosen for this sampler tray of proverbs.

Notice, first of all, that these proverbs all revolve around topics of *wisdom in public life*. There are no proverbs here about marriage or the family. There are no proverbs here about worship. Nor does the passage introduce any proverbs about righteousness, sin or other issues of morality. Attention is focused specifically on themes of wisdom in one's vocation or community relationships. Certainly, the repeated reference to folly includes sinful follies, but topics of morality are never explicitly addressed in this selection of sayings. These are all proverbs dealing with vocational and public affairs. Furthermore, these are proverbs that emphasize the importance of wisdom for the community, but with repeated reference to its limitations. The weakness of wisdom and its vulnerability to folly emerges frequently in this selection. Most importantly, the final proverb in the sequence exalts the sovereignty of God and his mysterious works over all the enigmas of human life.

This collection of proverbs does not form a coherent story. Nevertheless, taken together, these proverbs do present a coherent praise of wisdom for the health of Qohelet's kingdom. We might conclude that the passage has given us a photomosaic portrait of *modest wisdom* among those who live and work in the kingdom of David's son.

Call to joy (11:6–8)

The normal form of Qohelet's 'call to joy' is not here. There is no exhortation to 'eat and drink with joy' this time. Let's look at what is stated here, and then we will consider how it relates to the typical 'call to joy' we have come to expect at the end of each section.

These closing verses call us to rejoice by developing the imagery of light and darkness. 'In the morning sow your seed, and at evening withhold not your hand' (v. 6). A farmer does not limit his planting to the morning hours, supposing that morning seed is more likely to bloom than evening seed. Likewise, we are urged to continue exercising our gifts all through life, from the morning of life to the evening of life (v. 8).

Notice the exhortation to joy beginning to emerge in verses 7–8. Pleasure is natural when labouring in the sunshine (v. 7), but we are urged to rejoice in *all* our days, even knowing that many of them will be darkness, for 'All that comes is vanity [*hebel*, i.e. fleeting, enigmatic and fragile]' (v. 8). To rejoice through all the years of life—from sweet daylight to confusing darkness—is only possible when we rest in the sovereignty of God. No human wisdom can give certainty, but it is 'the work of God who makes everything' (v. 5). Only in that confidence can we live with joy all our days.

These closing verses do call us to rejoice: 'So if a person lives many years, let him rejoice in them all …' (v. 8). But this instruction is only a warm-up compared with the normal 'call to joy' repeated through Qohelet's book. This is probably because of the extended call to rejoice that follows in 11:9–12:8. 'Rejoice, O young man, in your youth, and let your heart cheer you in the days of your youth …' (v. 9). The closing call to joy for this section (9:11–11:8) is eclipsed by the extended word of joy (11:9–12:8) that forms the conclusion to the wisdom half of the book (6:10–12:8).

This is a similar arrangement to that found in the book of Psalms. As scholars have long noticed, the book of Psalms is organized into five parts, each ending with the doxology 'Blessed be the LORD, the God of Israel, from everlasting to everlasting! Amen and Amen' (Ps. 41:13; 72:18–19; 89:52; 106:48). The only exception is the ending of the last part of the book of Psalms, which has no such short doxology in its final psalm (Ps. 145). Instead, Psalms 146–150 serve as a grand doxology to close both the last section of the book and the entire Psalter. In a similar manner, the normal brief call to joy is lacking at the close of the final section of Ecclesiastes. Instead, a grand, overarching exhortation to 'Rejoice!' follows. We will take up this closing celebration of joy in the fear of the Lord in the next chapter.

Notes

1 Louise Élisabeth Vigée Le Brun, *Marie Antoinette and Her Children* (1787), Versailles.
2 See his website, www.photomosaic.com.
3 Murphy, *Ecclesiastes*, p. 105.
4 Cited in Fox, *A Time to Tear Down*, p. 312.

Rejoice! and remember! (11:9–12:8)

The seventeenth-century Dutch painter Ludolf Backhuysen took his art seriously. 'When the weather … [was] least favorable …,' one biographer wrote, 'he most loved to board a boat and sail to the mouth of the sea.'[1] Backhuysen wanted to see first-hand how the colours of the sky changed, the clouds swirled and the waters heaved as a storm stirred the ocean.

One of the results of his nature study is an impressive 1695 painting of a small fishing boat being helplessly tossed by a fierce storm at sea. The flag atop the boat's mast is torn, and its sails are straining in the wind with several ropes already snapped. Thick black clouds fill the sky, and mountainous waves chop the surface of the water. A few traces of sunlight over land on the distant horizon convey a sense of fading hope beyond reach of the sailors. It is a frightful tempest, painted with all the emotion the artist experienced weathering such storms himself.

But Backhuysen's masterpiece is actually a peaceful scene. The fishing boat in his painting is that of Peter, and seated at the back of the boat among the fearful disciples is the Lord of the sea and the waves. Backhuysen has painted the scene in such a way that a few rays of sunlight cut through the black clouds, casting light across the billowing waves on to the serene figure at the back of the boat. The painting—called *Christ in the Storm on the Sea of Galilee*—is a testament to the peace of Christ that is greater than the surrounding storm. The storm is there in all its fury; but peace reigns in its midst.

The book of Ecclesiastes is similar to Backhuysen's painting. Because most of the book's images capture the darkness of life's storms, the hopelessness of unreachable horizons and the tumult of uncertain waves, many readers assume that Ecclesiastes is a despairing book. But simply because the majority of the book's images are dismal does not mean that despair is its message. Like Backhuysen's storm framing the Lord of wind and waves, Ecclesiastes confronts life's tragedies in order to exult in the joy of those who fear God and rest in his sovereign grace.

Qohelet completes his lessons on wisdom with a resounding call to joy, even in the face of life's worst tragedy: death.

Rejoice! (11:9–10)

Qohelet brings his study of wisdom to a close with a grand call to rejoice. This has been the theme of his book: that living in the fear of God gives us grounds for joy despite the vanities of life. It is that very message that launches this conclusion at the end of his book. He calls us to rejoice in the knowledge of God's righteous judgement.

Unfortunately, most English Bibles cloud this point by how they translate a single conjunction near the end of verse 9. Most English Bibles translate the phrase about God's judgement in a manner that makes it sound like a threat, rather than a basis for pursuing joy. For example (all emphasis is added):

> Rejoice, O young man, in your youth, and let your heart cheer you in the days of your youth. Walk in the ways of your heart and the sight of your eyes. *But* know that for all these things God will bring you into judgement (ESV).

> Rejoice, young man, during your childhood, and let your heart be pleasant during the days of young manhood. And follow the impulses of your heart and the desires of your eyes. *Yet* know that God will bring you to judgment for all these things (NASB).

> Young people, it's wonderful to be young! Enjoy every minute of it. Do everything you want to do; take it all in. *But* remember that you must give an account to God for everything you do (NLT).

The Hebrew conjunction (*waw*) translated 'but' or 'yet' in the above

English versions could instead be translated 'and' or 'also'. The proper meaning of this Hebrew conjunction depends on its context. In this context, there is a string of seven commands, all of which are joined together by the exact same Hebrew conjunction, *waw*. Since each of the other commands in this sequence is an additional reason for rejoicing, there is no reason to translate the conjunction before the fifth command on the list differently from the rest—as though it is a threat ('but') in the middle of a list of cumulative ('and') reasons for joy. The seven commands in this grand call to rejoice are as follow:

1. Rejoice, young person, in your youth,
2. And (Heb. *waw*) let your heart cheer you in the days of your youth,
3. And (*waw*) walk in the ways of your heart,
4. And (*waw*) in the sight of your eyes,
5. And (*waw*) know that over all these matters, God will bring you into judgement,
6. And (*waw*) remove frustration from your heart,
7. And (*waw*) put away pain from your body, because youth and the prime of life are fleeting (*hebel*) (a.t.).[2]

Rather than reading the fifth command in this sequence (the command to keep God's judgement in mind) as the lone threat among otherwise happy invitations, we should actually see the instruction to fix our hearts on the certainty of God's judgement as the foundational assurance that undergirds the rest of the list. It is as we rest in the assurance of God's righteous judgement—that he *will* ultimately make all things right for us—that we are freed from the anxieties of life's present vanities.

It fits the context best to take Qohelet's call to rejoice seriously and unreservedly. There are no threats here that throw a wet towel over this building list of invitations to enjoy life. It is a grand, unreserved, glorious, even startlingly free invitation to pursue joy, grounded in the assurance we possess as those who fear the Lord.

Because the invitation to rejoice is so free and unqualified, many godly readers find it uncomfortable and imagine that there must be some restraint on this pursuit of pleasure. It is for this reason that the single line about God's judgement is so often translated in a manner that provides the restraint good Christian readers sense is needed. But we should recognize that the preceding chapters of the book already provide the restraint from foolish indulgence that is needed. As we come to this closing call to joy, we are not supposed to forget everything we have learned so far. With all the preceding lessons on wisdom and warnings of folly and the futility of rewards still in mind, Qohelet gives us this final call to pursue the best life has to offer. This is not a licentious permit to a life of indulgence; it is a bold welcome to enjoy life in the fear of the Lord.

When a judge delivers his ruling in court, that judgement pronounces 'bad news' for the guilty. But for the one who is vindicated, that exact same judgement is a word of reward and satisfaction. Throughout the Psalms, God's people (those who are living in reverence for his ways) anticipate his judgements and delight in them (e.g. Ps. 96; cf. Eccles. 8:12–13). Every Christian who looks forward to the Second Coming of Christ is taking hope in his judgement, when all wrongs will finally be purged and all the redeemed granted rest and eternal joy (e.g. Rev. 21:1–8). God's judgement is a threat only to those who despise his reign and ignore his commands. To those who have learned the faith taught in Ecclesiastes and throughout the Scriptures, God's judgement is an exciting prospect. God's judgement is the antidote to life's vanities.

Qohelet urges his readers—and especially young people—to take all that he is teaching to heart. He wants young people, in particular, to have the benefit of the wisdom that typically comes with the experience of age, but which he has provided for our instruction in this book. What a shame to wait until old age to have the understanding Qohelet wants us to capitalize on from youth!

'Youth and the prime of life are fleeting [*hebel*],' we are reminded (v. 10, a.t.). The strength of youth will not last for ever. This is not a threat, but a call to make the most of youthful strength while it lasts. Do not wait until the sorrows of old age to learn the joy of fearing God. Qohelet is urging young people to set aside the frivolous pleasures of godlessness and instead to give themselves all their days to that joy of life that is grounded in the fear of the Lord.

Remember! (12:1–7)

Nowadays, when the sun sets and the sky darkens, we flick the light switch and continue our work. Modern life is no longer tied to the rising and setting of the sun in the way it used to be. But imagine a time when sunset meant the unavoidable end of the workday. Recognizing the approach of sunset provided impetus to pick up the pace and work diligently to finish. Actually, the prudent worker would start the day with knowledge of the coming sunset. Even when the morning sun was just rising and the day ahead seemed endless, knowing that sunset would eventually come gave impetus to employ the whole day wisely (and avoid a last-minute crisis at the end).

Modern lighting allows us to lengthen our 'daylight' hours, and modern medicine also offers us many opportunities to delay death. But the end is still out there. All through Ecclesiastes, Qohelet has repeatedly identified the inevitability and unfairness of death as the ultimate demonstration of life's fundamental vanity. At the end of the book, he takes up the great evil of death and calls us to face it head-on. Even in youth, we must not ignore but rather recognize the coming of death. However, the reason Qohelet closes his book with a poem about death is not to be morbid or to lead us to despair; he tells us that a recognition of the coming darkness drives us to 'remember our Creator' even in youth (v. 1). Let's look more closely at how this poem on death strengthens our hope in the Creator in life.

First of all, we need to clarify what this poem in Ecclesiastes 12:1–8 is actually about. Clearly, it is a poem about the approach of death. But what are these word pictures Qohelet strings together into this poem that stirs us to take death seriously? Some commentators think the poem describes an approaching storm.[3] The opening references to clouds and rain (v. 2) are taken as the introduction of a devastating storm approaching the community. 'The destruction from the storm that looms for the community', Daniel Fredericks explains, '[is] … a metaphor for the destruction of the aged's body …'[4] Other interpreters understand the poem to be a collection of metaphors on the varied burdens of ageing and death.[5] These are possibilities; however, it seems to me that the best interpretation discussed among commentators is that the poem describes the end of life and the subsequent funeral procession.[6]

Qohelet strings together a series of snapshots of a man's last journey on earth 'to his eternal home' (v. 5) as his 'dust returns to the earth' and his 'spirit returns to God' (v. 7). This interpretation of the poem allows the statement at the end of verse 5 to serve as the poem's own explanation of what is taking place: the preceding scenes of grief occur 'because a man is going to his eternal home, and the mourners are gathering in the streets' (a.t.). Read the following translation of this ancient Hebrew funeral poem, after which I will make some observations about the poem and then discuss its role in Qohelet's exhortation to 'Remember the Creator':

[1]Remember your Creator
in the days of your youth—
Before the evil days come and the years arrive
when you say, 'There is no pleasure in them for me';
[2]before the sun and (its) light grows dark,
and the moon and the stars,
and the clouds return after the rain.
[3]In the days when the keepers of the house tremble,
and strong men stoop over,
and the grinding-maids cease for dwindling numbers,
and the watching-women in the windows darken,

[4]and the gates in the streets are closed

in the fading sound of the grinding-mill.

Then the birds rise to sing,

and all the daughters of song are bowed low.

[5]Also they fear things on high and terrors in the way,

and the almond tree blossoms, and the locust (tree) grows laden,

and the caper berry (bush) buds.

For the man is going to his eternal home,

and the mourners are gathering in the streets.

[6]Before the silver cord is snapped,

and the golden bowl is smashed,

and the pitcher is shattered at the spring,

and the wheel is broken in the pit,

[7]and the dust returns to the earth as it was before,

and the breath returns to God who gave it.

The moral of the poem is to 'remember [our] Creator' (v. 1), and to do so *before* we come to the brink of death. The importance of doing so *before* death is stated twice. We are told in verses 1–5 to remember our Creator '*before* the evil days [of ageing and death] …' Then the word 'before' is repeated in verse 6, introducing a second exhortation in verses 6–7 to remember the Creator '*before* the silver cord [of life] is snapped …' It is the first of the two 'before [death]' sections that describes a man's dying days and funeral procession to the grave.

Verses 1–2 use a series of images of darkness to capture the gloom of a man's final days when life holds no more pleasure. We recall that Qohelet's previous exhortation was to rejoice and find pleasure in life (11:9–10). There are days coming when pleasure will be lost. It is a poetic allusion to the season of decline approaching death.

In verses 3–4, death has occurred and the community's grief is described. The writer uses a technique similar to that of many modern movies. He begins by capturing the reactions of the household and of the surrounding community. It is like a movie that reveals that the hero has died by showing us his family in black and their weeping, only later turning the cameras to the deceased himself. In a similar manner, Qohelet first describes the household staff grieving, the working men bowed over, and both the working women and the older women of the household in sorrow. Grinding wheat for each day's bread was a typical task of women in a Hebrew household. Verse 3 covers all corners of the household, from the strong men who labour in the fields to the young women grinding grain, to the older women darkening the windows as they all turn their attention to what is passing through the streets. Verse 4 completes the description of the household with the courtyard gates closing as the sounds of the grinding mills are falling silent. Work is coming to a standstill, and the labourers are all leaving their posts.

According to the first-century Jewish historian Josephus, ancient Hebrew burials were community affairs. The family carried the deceased to the tomb, and 'all who pass by when a corpse is being buried must accompany the funeral and join in the lamentations'.[7] The New Testament also describes such a procession with the deceased carried on a bier, and the passing crowds, including Jesus, joining (Luke 7:11–17). Qohelet's poem seems to take place in such a procession.

In the final images of verses 4 and 5, a series of stunning contrasts is introduced. The rising songs of birds are contrasted with the low lamentations of songstresses.[8] Also, the surrounding fears experienced by all are contrasted with the surrounding foliage bursting into bloom. This is one of the most intriguing features of Qohelet's poem, for he has chosen to frame this day of death in the season of springtime and new life.

This translation of verse 5 (with blossoming trees and bushes) is different from that found in most English Bibles. For example, the ESV translates verse 5, '... the almond tree blossoms, the grasshopper drags itself along, and desire fails ...' Many translators think the blossoming of the almond tree is an allusion to the greying of an old man's hair. The 'locust' mentioned is thought to be the insect by that name rather than the locust *tree,* and a 'laden locust' is thought to evoke images of a grasshopper dragging its feet. The grasshopper is, so the thinking goes, a poetic image for an old man who is partially lame. Likewise, the reference to the 'opening (or breaking) caper berry' is thought to be a euphemistic reference to failing desire (the caper berry being regarded as an aphrodisiac which fails to help). But the most natural interpretation of these agricultural terms is that of springtime scenery.[9] Perhaps because the poem is an image of death, translators find it jolting to encounter imagery of cheerful birds and springtime blossoms in verses 4–5; hence the tendency to strain these nature images into references to old age. But the springtime imagery actually fits remarkably well. It reminds us of the Creator as the giver of life. It sets a context for the poem that faces all the horror of death, but not in a manner that loses all sense of beauty and hope.

It is at the end of verse 5 that the cameras pull back to reveal the overall scene. After the preceding series of snapshots of grief at springtime, the final lines of verse 5 show the reason for these sorrows. It is 'because the man [of this household] is going to his eternal home, and the mourners are gathering in the streets' (a.t.).

The scene of the funeral procession is finished, and at this point Qohelet's exhortation intensifies. The word 'before' at the start of verse 6 brings our thoughts back to the main instruction of the passage. This is not a passage about death, but about our lives *before* the approach of death. The 'before' at the start of verse 6 reminds us that Qohelet's instruction is to 'Remember your Creator ... *before*' these things happen.

Verse 6 describes the moment of death with a series of metaphors: the silver cord snapping, the golden bowl breaking, the (clay) pitcher shattering at the spring, and the wheel (used to draw water from the well) broken in the well. These are images that remind us that valuable tools (those of silver and gold) and common tools (pitchers and the cistern wheels) alike come to their demise.[10] In this world of fleeting uncertainty, everything eventually fails. Likewise, human flesh returns to dust, and human breath is ultimately taken by God (v. 7). All the world is marked by fleetingness (v. 8).

This is a poem to sober us, but not to depress us. Like Backhuysen's stormy sea painting, Qohelet's funeral poem sets death before us as a backdrop for his call to rejoice in life—but to do so in the fear of the Lord. We must join our rejoicing with remembering the Creator.

Notice how Qohelet speaks of God by his title 'Creator' at the opening of the passage. Then he concludes his poem in language clearly drawn from the biblical creation account (cf. Eccles. 12:7 with Gen. 2:7). It is no coincidence that we are reminded to remember God under his title 'Creator' in this passage. It was the Creator who formed man from dust and breathed into him the breath of life. It is the same Creator, Qohelet shows us, who is sovereign over the return of dust to the ground and of breath (or man's spirit) to God's possession.

It is possible that the springtime imagery in the poem is a further subtle reference to our hope in the Creator as the one who is sovereign over life. Peoples throughout the ancient world regarded spring as an indication that the creator of the world was a god of rebirth. Even the Canaanite Baal rituals grasped a rudimentary, shadowy understanding of this point from the testimony of each year's summer drought followed by life-giving rain and spring fertility.[11] The annual festivals of Old Testament Israel also seemed to capture this hope. The worship calendar of Israel aligned remembrance of God's deliverance from the Angel of Death (Passover) with the annual festival of springtime (Lev. 23:4–8).[12] Most commentators think that Qohelet's references to spring in this poem are to underscore the tragedy of death; but perhaps there is more to it. Perhaps these elements of spring renewal are subtle allusions to the life-giving nature of the Creator whom we are told to remember.

Whatever hints and allusions to hope Qohelet may have woven into the poem, he never makes that hope explicit in the poem. After all, the point of this lyric is to alert us to the reality of death as the end of human pleasure (under the sun). The purpose of the poem is to confront us with the sobering reality of death. But the reason it does so is to stir us to trust our Creator, even in the expectation of death. This funeral song is not here to pull the rug out from under Qohelet's earlier call to rejoice (11:9–10). Rather, the remembrance of our Creator in anticipation of death provides the context of godly fear for guiding our joy.

Fear God; remember the Creator; and in that faith, make the most of life's joys!

All is vanity (12:8)

The admission that closes the final section of the book is the same admission that opened the beginning of the book: 'Vanity of vanities, says the Preacher; all is vanity' (v. 8; so also 1:2). The author ends with the same admission with which he began. But in between these bookends, our teacher has instructed us to pursue godly joy, and how to do so.

Actually, there is a particular audience Qohelet is addressing in this book. *Young people* are the special focus of these lessons (11:9; 12:1). Certainly, young and old alike will benefit from Ecclesiastes; but the book is especially aimed at youth. What a timely word this book brings for youth today!

Western culture is fascinated with the period of adolescence. In the modern West, adolescence is the period in life when young people have the physical development and many of the capacities and economic resources of adulthood, but few of the responsibilities of adulthood. Youth is idealized as the period of life to pursue pleasure, and adolescence is prolonged as long as possible.[13] The world is urging young people to pursue pleasure, ignoring God and ignoring death.

Qohelet gives more realistic advice. Death, and all the rest of life's vanities, cannot be ignored. And they should not be ignored. However, admitting life's uncertainties and enigmas does not have to leave us living in fear and despair. And contrary to the misconceptions of the world, remembering God in youth is not a killjoy doctrine. Instead, it is revering God that enables young people to rejoice without ignoring life's troubles!

Ecclesiastes may be written in ancient Hebrew using old-world metaphors and archaic terminology, but its message is up-to-date and relevant for young people facing the uncertainties of the twenty-first century.

Notes

1 Arnold Houbraken, quoted on the plaque beside Ludolf Backhuysen, *Christ in the Storm on the Sea of Galilee*, 1695, at the Indianapolis Museum of Art.

2 Notably, the oldest translation of the Hebrew Bible (the Septuagint translation into Greek, done around 200 BC) translates all the conjunctions in this passage as 'and' (Greek *kai*). The Latin Vulgate (c. AD 382) also translates all the conjunctions with 'and' (Latin *et*). Cf. the English translation from the Vulgate, the Douay-Rheims (1582), which translates with the English 'and'.

3 E.g. Fredericks, 'Ecclesiastes', pp. 231–243.

4 E.g. Fredericks, 'Ecclesiastes', p. 233.

5 E.g. Delitzsch, *Commentary on The Song of and Songs and Ecclesiastes*, pp. 401–426; cf. Thomas Krüger, *Qoheleth: A Commentary* (trans. O. C. Dean; Hermeneia 21; Minneapolis: Fortress Press, 2004), pp. 198–204.

6 E.g. Murphy, *Ecclesiastes*, pp. 114–122; Fox, *A Time to Tear Down*, pp. 333–349.

7 Josephus, *Against Apion*, 2.205.

8 The poetic line about the bird literally says, 'He rises to sound, the bird' (*weyaqum leqol hatsippor*). Some translators understand this to refer to a person being startled by the sound of a bird (e.g. ESV). However, it also could be the bird (or, in this case, the noun might be used collectively for birds in general) *rising* to sing. The latter interpretation seems to fit the poetry better, producing a contrast of the rising of the birds' song with the *lowness* of the songstresses' laments (cf. Fox, *A Time to Tear Down*, pp. 325–326).

9 Fox, *A Time to Tear Down*, pp. 327–328; cf. Murphy, *Ecclesiastes*, p. 119.

10 Particularly striking is the location of the final two items. The 'spring' (where the pitcher breaks) is a metaphor for a source of life (e.g. Isa. 35:7) and the 'pit' (into which the cistern wheel falls) is the same word used for the grave (e.g. Isa. 14:15).

11 In the Canaanite Baal rituals, 'through the summer months Death and the destructive forces reigned supreme … The rains begin again in the fall … [because] Baal comes back to life … [and] verdure cover[s] the land in the spring …' (G. Ernest Wright, *Biblical Archaeology* (Philadelphia: Westminster Press, 1966), p. 111).

12 Cf. Roy Gane, *Leviticus, Numbers* (NIVAC; Grand Rapids: Zondervan, 2009), pp. 393–395; John Hartley, *Leviticus* (WBC 4; Dallas: Word Books, 1992), pp. 393–394. Note also the ancient Christian tradition of replacing Passover with Easter.

13 For an interesting analysis of the modern pursuit of perpetual adolescence, see Diana West, *The Death of the Grown-Up: How America's Arrested Development Is Bringing Down Western Civilization* (New York: St Martin's Griffin, 2008).

Epilogue: the sum of the matter (12:9–14)

hen a Special Forces unit is sent on a mission, it is first briefed about the mission. In a secret meeting, the soldiers are oriented to the objectives and obstacles of their task. After the mission is over, the soldiers are debriefed. Debriefing is a time to review how the mission went, whether the objectives were met and what lessons were learned.

The prologue and epilogue framing the book of Ecclesiastes are like briefing and debriefing sessions. In the prologue (1:1–18), we were given a 'map' for the examination of life's vanities on which the book led us. At the other end of the book, the epilogue (12:9–14) reviews what we have just studied and helps us to distil the primary lesson.

Summing up what we've read (12:9–12)

Two titles of Israel's king are used in this short passage. He is called 'Qohelet' (vv. 9–10; translated as 'the Preacher' in most English Bibles) and 'Shepherd' (v. 11). Both of these are royal titles that reflect the king's duties to care for the people. We saw at the beginning of this book that 'Qohelet' means 'assembler'. It is the title ascribed to a ruler who gathers the people to instruct them in the face of a social crisis. 'Shepherd' is another title that describes the king's duty as one responsible for caring for the people as a herder tends his sheep.

In these closing lines of the book, we are led to consider the love of the king whose voice ministers to us through Ecclesiastes. Originally, it was Solomon, the wisest of Israel's ancient kings, who compiled this book. But the book was not retired at the end of Solomon's reign. Successive generations of kings continued to hold out the words of this book as royal wisdom for the people. This book became part of the canonical wisdom of the Hebrew kings. Ultimately, it is Jesus, the greatest Son of David, who takes up the canonical wisdom books of the covenant kingdom and speaks in them to us. Truly, it is for our guidance and our shepherding care that this book continues to speak to the church.

The first two verses of this passage (vv. 9–10) review the faithful work of the Qohelet ('Preacher') in this book we have just read. He was a king endowed by God with great wisdom, and he did not keep that wisdom to himself. He employed his wisdom to undertake the examinations reported in this book, distilling all his findings to the choicest of proverbs and doctrines for our edification. The 'knowledge' and 'many proverbs' that verse 9 says Qohelet arranged 'with great care' is a reference to the wisdom sayings compiled into the book just completed. Verse 10 sums up the character of the resulting distillation. Ecclesiastes is a book containing 'words of delight, and ... words of truth'.

In the operating room of a hospital, there will inevitably be a lot of cutting, blood, and perhaps tumours or other revolting discoveries. But the overall procedure, carried out with wisdom and precision, is one of healing and wholeness. Likewise, Ecclesiastes has led us through many cancerous plagues of life's vanities, but the guidance provided ministers truth and delight to our hearts. These truly are 'words of delight, and ... truth'.

The next two verses (vv. 11–12) encourage us to take to heart these words and to live by them, as sheep cared for by the true Shepherd. Verse 11 likens the words of this book to goads and nails. A goad is a farmer's staff with a sharp tip used to prod cattle while leading them. The tip may hurt a bit, for it is sharp. But unlike that of an instrument of attack (such as a spear), the purpose of the goad is to protect from wrong turns and to guide in the right way. Likewise, when our Shepherd 'goads' us with convicting words, it is for our good. Nails (or pegs), in ancient times as in modern, are used to secure things in place. This collection of lessons is fixed and trustworthy: 'like nails firmly fixed are the collected sayings [in this book]' (v. 11).

The epilogue is urging us to embrace the philosophy of life provided in this book above all others. There are countless other sages who have written (and who continue to write, even today) books to help people make sense of life's vanities. Some are good, some are not. But Ecclesiastes is the exposition of life's vanities by which all others are to be tested, because this is the collection given to us by our 'one Shepherd' (v. 11). By calling our king the '*one* Shepherd', the point is being made that our whole allegiance is to this one alone. We could translate the phrase 'our only Shepherd' to get at its meaning. All other allegiances are secondary to this one.

This book is, therefore, the authorized text on making sense of life's vanities. We are thus urged, 'My son, beware of anything beyond these [words]. Of making many books there is no end, and much study is a weariness of the flesh' (v. 12). This is not censorship; it is a word of caution. As Christians, we can find much benefit from reading the observations of different authors who write about culture and its problems. The epilogue of Ecclesiastes is not instigating a book-burning event. In fact, verse 12 acknowledges that there is lots of room for writing many more books beyond what is said in Ecclesiastes, and it might even be taken as an endorsement for more studies of life's vanities. However, as subjects of this Shepherd, we are to weigh all other books against the teachings we find here. This one is adequate. It covers all the essential bases.

With the reading of this book, we can cease our fretting over life's frailties and enigmas. 'Much study is a weariness of the flesh' (v. 12). Our Shepherd has distilled the sum of the matter in this book for us, so we can relax, rest in his guidance, and pursue our life's work with vigour and joy.

Summing up what we've learned (12:13–14)

We have encountered many doctrines and proverbs in Ecclesiastes. We now come to the final maxim of the book. It is the sum of the matter, distilling everything into one clear conclusion. We might call this 'the one proverb to rule them all'.

Many well-meaning Christian teachers promote biblical morality because, they say, doing things God's way will make life happier and make us more successful. Qohelet also calls us to trust God, to worship and revere him by obeying his ways; but the reason to do so is not because God's ways guarantee us greater success. The reason to do so is simple: he is God and we are human. It is our created purpose to honour him, stewarding our lives and the world according to his purposes.

Our faithfulness to his ways may *not* bring good results in this life under the sun. Yet we know that 'God will bring every deed into judgement, with every secret thing, whether good or evil' (v. 14). Even though obeying his ways may *not* 'work' during this vain life under the sun, we can be absolutely confident that honouring his ways *will* bring great reward at the last.

Scholars often debate whether the author of Ecclesiastes had an expectation of the afterlife. The reason why students of Ecclesiastes ask that question is because the book never says anything explicit about life after death, but it does say a lot about the finality of death. Therefore, many commentators think that Ecclesiastes is a book with a dim view of life and no concept of an afterlife.

There is, however, a massive hole in that perspective. The examination reported throughout the book is, by explicit design, an examination of life 'under the sun'. That is all that is available for examination of the kind undertaken in this book. Furthermore, the repeated finding of the book is that there is no certain justice 'under the sun'. Nevertheless, repeatedly through its pages we are brought back to a foundation of confidence that God will ultimately provide a final accounting and will award justice—and that we will participate in that reward. The closing line anchors the whole book upon that confidence.

The encouragement Qohelet ministers to our souls through this book is the same joy triumphantly proclaimed by the Apostle Paul: 'When the perishable puts on the imperishable, and the mortal puts on immortality, then shall come to pass the saying that is written: "Death is swallowed up in victory." … Therefore, my beloved brothers, be steadfast, immovable, always abounding in the work of the Lord, knowing that *in the Lord your labour is not in vain*' (1 Cor. 15:54, 58, emphasis added).

Perhaps the Apostle Paul had the book of Ecclesiastes—with its exposition of life's vanities—in mind when he penned that reminder that, in the Lord, our labours are 'not in vain'. But whether or not Paul was thinking about Ecclesiastes, he was expressing the same faith.

Pursue wisdom. Grow in grace. Seek productive and fruitful labours. But knowing life's inherent vanities, let your joy be in God's sovereign grace, regardless of what confusion life throws your way. 'In the Lord your labour is *not* in vain.'